CAST THY NETS

CAST THY NETS

The Power of Love & Discipleship

ERIC STENGEL

HEART OF
A LION PUBLISHING

Cast Thy Nets: The Power of Love & Discipleship

Cover Design: Courtesy of HMDPublishing.com
Artwork: Courtesy of Allison Hsu, Christine Barrantes, Angela Stengel,
Public Domain images curated and adapted by Eric Stengel
Book formatting: Creative Publishing Book Design

Published by: Heart of a Lion Consulting Richardson, Texas, USA

Scripture quotations taken from the Saint Joseph
Edition of the New American Bible (NAB).
Used with permission. All rights reserved.

Printed in the United States of America.
First Edition, 2025

Contents

Preface

Beginning a task as significant as authoring a book is never easy. Yet the gentle urging of the Holy Spirit moved me to begin, with one goal: to give all glory to God. Through the intercession of my confirmation saint, St. Mark the Evangelist, I found the courage to set pen to paper.

My deepest hope is that this book draws readers closer to Jesus Christ, the Second Person of the Holy Trinity. If even one person discovers a new perspective on his walk of faith, then this work will have borne fruit.

As a husband and father, I have come to see that love is more than a feeling or a word; it is a verb. When Jesus asked Peter, "Simon, son of John, do you love me more than these?" He immediately followed that question by entrusting Peter with a mission: "Feed my lambs. Tend my sheep. Feed my sheep."[1] Love reveals itself in action given and received and finds its fullest expression in vocation.

The word vocation, from the Latin vocare, "to call," has a twofold meaning for me. My first and primary vocation is to live as a disciple of Jesus Christ. Flowing from this is my second vocation: to be a

---

[1] Jn. 21:15

devoted husband and a caring father to my daughter. Just as Jesus is the true manna come down from Heaven, nourishing us with the grace of the Holy Spirit, so too are we called to nurture one another in every encounter.

This call to live love as action is the deepest motivation for this work, born of personal encounters with Christ and shaped by the daily call to embody His love within my family and beyond.

LED BY THE SPIRIT

Each of us is guided by the Holy Spirit along life's journey, just as the Apostles were led at Pentecost, when the Church was born. The One, Holy, Catholic, and Apostolic Church is the vessel Christ established to strengthen and sustain us as we journey toward heaven.

Each time we profess the Creed, we affirm that the Church founded by Jesus Christ is One, Holy, Catholic, and Apostolic. These four marks are not abstract ideas; they describe who the Church is and how she lives out Christ's mission in the world.

The Church is One because she is united in Jesus Christ. This unity spans all cultures, generations, and backgrounds. It calls us to set aside pride, seek reconciliation, and walk together in humility as members of one Body.

The Church is Holy because Christ Himself is holy and continues to sanctify her. Through the sacraments, especially the Eucharist and Reconciliation, God pours out His grace upon us. Although her members are imperfect and in constant need of conversion, the Church remains holy because Christ is always at work within her.

The Church is Catholic, meaning universal. She embraces people of every nation, language, and way of life. Like a wide net cast into the sea, the Church gathers all who are open to God's grace. United in faith through the Roman Rite and the Eastern rites, the Church is guided by the successor of Saint Peter, the Pope, who serves as a sign of unity among the faithful.

The Church is Apostolic because she is built upon the foundation of the apostles. Their witness has been faithfully handed on through Sacred Tradition, Sacred Scripture, and the teaching authority of the Church. We share in this apostolic mission when we live the Gospel and bear witness to Christ in our daily lives.

Through the sacraments, God continually nourishes and renews His people. Grace unfolds according to God's timing, not our own. While we cannot relive the past, we honor it, for our Catholic faith is rooted in the faithful witness of those who have gone before us and now encourage us to persevere on our journey of faith.

The call of discipleship is simple yet profound: remain open to Christ's presence in worship, prayer, work, school, family life, and leisure. In every circumstance, Jesus is there. He is the way, the truth, and the life (Jn. 14:6). Like Job, who clung to faith amid suffering, we too must trust that God is guiding us.

A PERSONAL JOURNEY

Our family has known both joy and trial. Some of our loved ones have drifted from active participation in the Church, yet they remain members of Christ's Body, forever marked by the indelible seal of baptism (cf. CCC 1272). I was reminded of this truth when Angela and I were invited to be godparents at our niece's baptism. In that moment, we experienced a quiet reunion of faith, drawn together by Christ's love.

Baptism is more than a ritual. It signifies new life, removes original sin, and anoints with the Spirit. Each time I see the flame of a baptismal candle, I am reminded that the light of Christ burns within us all.

THE CALL OF DISCIPLESHIP

Remaining active in our parish community and participating in sacramental life has been a source of joy for my family. But God's plan is not just for me or my household; it is for each one of us. Scripture reminds us that the roads we travel are part of His divine plan (cf. Exod. 33:12; Ps. 27:11). The question is: will we follow where He leads?

That is the heart of this book. Cast Thy Nets: The Power of Love and Discipleship is an invitation from the Master Fisherman. He casts His net wide, longing to draw us in. Our task is simple: to trust, to believe, and to allow ourselves to be caught in His love and follow Him.

Prologue

Paschal Candle from my Niece Evie's Baptism.
A Reminder that the Light of Christ Dwells in Us
(Photo Credit: Eric Stengel)

The inspiration for this book comes from a powerful moment in John's Gospel. After the Resurrection, the disciples fished all night without success. Their nets were empty, their spirits weary, their mission uncertain.

Then a stranger appeared on the shore and called out, "Cast the net on the right side of the boat, and you will find some."[1] They obeyed, and suddenly their nets overflowed with fish. The Beloved Disciple recognized the stranger and exclaimed, "It is the Lord!"[2]

This moment speaks to the very heart of Christian life: trust, obedience, and transformation. Jesus' invitation was not only about fish; it was about faith.

A CALL THAT ECHOES TODAY

Like the disciples, we too are invited to trust the voice that calls us from the distant shore. Jesus' words reach across time, calling us to trust even when we feel exhausted, discouraged, or uncertain.

For the disciples, listening to Jesus and daring to try again opened the door to a life-changing encounter. For us, it can be the same: a gentle invitation to trust and to begin again when our prayers seem to fall silent or when our hearts feel empty. The miracle assures us that Jesus is never far. He walks beside us, even when we do not recognize Him, always ready to renew our hope and fill us with His grace.

LETTING DOWN THE NETS EACH DAY

Casting the net was a rhythmic action for a fisherman. In our lives of faith, casting the net is the rhythm of discipleship. Each act of love and trust makes space for God's grace.

---

[1] Jn. 21:6
[2] Jn. 21:7

Our "nets" are the choices we make daily to trust Him:

> To forgive when it is difficult.
>
> To pray when our hearts feel dry.
>
> To offer love when it costs something.

INVITATION TO RENEWAL

This book is an invitation to the same journey. Just as the disciples' obedience brought abundance, so too our surrender to Christ brings the richness of faith.

The question is not whether Jesus is present; He is. The question is whether we are willing to trust His timing, His guidance, and His love enough to keep casting our nets.

This is not only the story of the apostles, but also our story.

Chapter One

Deep Waters Deeper Faith

Appearance on Lake Tiberias, Duccio di Buoninsegna, 14th century.
Depicts Jesus and the seven disciples (with Saint Peter leaving the boat)
in the scene of the miraculous catch of 153 fish. Public domain image.

ENTERING THE DEEP

Faith can feel like stepping into deep water. Some days we hesitate on the shore; other days we dive in, trusting that God will carry us. I have lived both realities, including seasons of distance and doubt after leaving seminary, drifting from the Mass, and exploring other traditions, convinced that sincerity was enough. While many Protestant and nondenominational communities offer excellent exegesis on the Word of God and cultivate vibrant praise and worship, I gradually realized something was missing: Jesus, truly present, body, blood, soul and divinity in the Holy Eucharist. That realization, together with the humble invitation of a parish priest at the nearby Catholic university parish, is what led me home.

A WELCOME BACK

One day, I felt drawn back to St. Elizabeth Catholic University Parish. What greeted me was not a grand sermon, but the simple kindness of a priest. Fr. Bill shook my hand, smiled, and welcomed me back. Through him, I felt Jesus reaching out again.

Years later, reading Fr. Bill's obituary, I discovered his favorite prayer from St. John Henry Newman:

May He support us all the day long, till the shades lengthen and the evening comes, and the busy world is hushed, and the fever of life is over, and our work is done. Then in His mercy may He give us a safe lodging, and a holy rest, and peace at the last.[1]

---

[1] John Henry Newman, *Meditations and Devotions* (London: Longmans, Green, and Co., 1893), 301.

Those words remind me that faith is not a sprint but a daily walk with Christ, even when the waters run deep.

SENT INTO THE WORLD

At the end of Mass, the priest says, "Ite, missa est," meaning, "Go forth, you are sent." Fr. Bill's welcoming presence before Mass reminds us that grace-filled encounters and moments of discipleship are not meant to stay within church walls; they are meant to send us out into a world marked by doubt and distraction and bring the truth and light of Christ to others. In carrying forward the apostolic tradition handed down from Saint Peter and the first apostles, the Church continues Christ's mission through us. This mission is now our own.

Like Peter on the shore of Galilee, Jesus asks each of us, "Do you love me?"[2] However we answer, His invitation remains the same: "Follow Me."[3]

WOUNDED, YET LOVED

Some carry wounds of judgment, betrayal, and neglect from the Church. Others drift away quietly. If that is your story, hear this truth: you are not alone, and God's love has never wavered. We are made for love and God's Church is the vessel through which that love is lived and shared if only we have the courage to surrender to the invitation of Jesus' boundless love for us. When the evil one comes knocking at our door, we should remember the words of Matthew's Gospel when Jesus proclaims Peter to be the rock upon which His Church shall be built. Christ emphasizes that the gates of Hell shall

---

[2] Jn. 21:15-17
[3] Jn. 21:19

not prevail against this Church, through which He is performing His redemptive work of love for the world. (Mt 16:18).

Later, when Peter sees Jesus on the shore, he leaps into the water, unprepared and imperfect. Yet Jesus meets him with love. God asks the same response of us, not polished perfection, but a sincere heart. As the prophet Joel says, "Rend your hearts, not your garments."[4]

ANCHORED IN GRACE AND SACRAMENTS

The saints knew this truth well. St. Augustine confessed, "Our hearts are restless until they rest in You."[5] Teresa of Ávila, John of the Cross, and St. John Henry Newman all wrestled with doubts and failures, yet they rowed into the deep waters with trust.

Perseverance is anchored in the sacraments. The Eucharist strengthens us. Reconciliation heals us. These are not empty rituals; they are encounters with Christ Himself, who takes our "empty nets" and fills them with grace.

Faith cannot remain a spectator sport. The Holy Spirit moves us from simply going through the motions to living with purpose:

Forgiveness over bitterness.

Compassion over cynicism.

Trust over fear.

As St. Paul reminds us: "Vengeance is mine, says the Lord."[6] Forgiveness, on the other hand clears space for grace. When we forgive, we begin to live like Christ, becoming a light for others.

---

[4] Jl. 2:13

[5] Augustine. *Confessions*. Translated by Henry Chadwick. Oxford: Oxford University Press, 1991, 3.

[6] Rom. 12:19

A FAMILY OF DISCIPLES

The journey to sainthood is both personal and communal. Each of us struggles, but none of us walks alone. The Body of Christ is a family united by His love. Faith means supporting each other and relying on grace together.

REFLECTION QUESTIONS FROM CHAPTER ONE

Why am I a Catholic Christian?

Where am I still holding back from God's net?

Am I willing, like Peter, to say, "Yes, Lord, you know that I love you"?

ACTION STEP: TAKE THE NEXT STEP INTO THE DEEP

This week, choose one concrete way to "cast your net" deeper with Christ:

Return – If you've been away from Mass or Reconciliation, set a date this week to go. Walk back into His mercy.

Renew – If you already attend Mass regularly, consider adding one intentional step: arrive early to pray, participate in daily Mass once, or spend fifteen minutes in Eucharistic Adoration.

Reach Out – As Fr. Bill did by welcoming me, offer a simple gesture of kindness or invitation to someone who seems distant from the Church. A smile, a coffee invitation, or a word of encouragement can be the net that brings this person closer to Jesus.

Pray Simply – End each day with the prayer of the tax collector: "O God, have mercy on me, a sinner."[7] Let those words anchor you in humility and grace.

Faith is not about diving in perfectly; it is about stepping in again, one act of trust at a time.

---

[7] Lk. 18:13

Chapter Two

Swimming Toward Our Mission

Baptismal font, St. Joseph Church, Richardson.
Reborn in Christ and freed from original sin.
Photo by Eric Stengel.

THE STRUGGLE OF SWIMMING UPSTREAM

Faith can feel like swimming against a strong current: no matter how hard we push, we end up exhausted. We attend Mass, pray when we can, and volunteer, yet often keep our faith separate from work, family, or finances. Instead of having one

integrated life in Christ, we live in compartments. I have done this myself, sharing victories like a social media highlight reel while hiding struggles. But the Christian life is not about keeping God in a box; it is about letting Him into everything, even the messy parts.

AT THE CENTER: THE CROSS AND BAPTISM

At the center of our faith stands the Cross. Jesus said, "If anyone would come after me, let him deny himself, take up his cross, and follow me."[1] This is the Paschal Mystery, the Passion, Death, and Resurrection of Christ, made present at every Mass. It teaches us that discipleship is not about comfort but about a love that costs something. We cannot skip Good Friday and still reach Easter Sunday.

Baptism makes this real. At my parish, the font is shaped like both a womb and a tomb because, in baptism, we both die to sin and are reborn as children of God (CCC 1265). It is a grace that never leaves us, even when life gets messy.

LIVING THE MISSION TODAY

Discipleship is lived daily, whether in marriage, the priesthood, religious life, or single life, by carrying burdens with Christ's love and showing quiet generosity.

---

[1] Mt. 16:24

In marriage, spouses generously carry one another's burdens with Christ's love. In the priesthood or religious life, vows reflect the total and continual gift of self. In single life, holiness is found in quiet generosity toward family, friends, and neighbors.

As the Church teaches in the document Lumen Gentium, "All the faithful of Christ of whatever rank or status are called to the fullness of the Christian life and to the perfection of charity."[2] Holiness is not perfectionism; it is showing up, carrying your cross, and loving well.

The 153 fish the disciples caught on the Sea of Tiberias—a tremendous number—indicate variety, reminding us that the Church is for everyone of all nations, vocations, and stages of life. No matter what one's situation, when your net feels empty, Jesus says, "Cast again. Trust Me."

Even Peter, who denied Jesus, was restored with this simple but profound question: "Do you love me?" Peter's yes healed him. Ours can too.

OUR INVITATION: BECOMING THE HANDS AND FEET OF CHRIST

In a noisy, divided world, Jesus' question to Peter remains His question to us: "Do you love me more than these?"[3] Discipleship begins with simple steps:

- Placing one part of your life into God's hands today.
- Praying sincerely, even in a single "Yes, Lord."
- Choosing forgiveness, compassion, and trust over bitterness, cynicism, and fear.

---

[2] Second Vatican Council. *Lumen Gentium* [Dogmatic Constitution on the Church]. In *Vatican Council II: The Conciliar and Post Conciliar Documents*, edited by Austin Flannery, O.P., 1–75. Northport, NY: Costello Publishing, 1996. §40.
[3] Jn. 21:15

Saint Teresa of Ávila is said to have penned this prayer oftentimes attributed to her

"Christ has no body now but yours, no hands, no feet on earth but yours. Yours are the eyes through which He looks with compassion upon this world."[4]

Every act of love—raising children, caring for the sick, forgiving, etc.—becomes God's mission. It begins here, in your life.

REFLECTION QUESTIONS FROM CHAPTER TWO

What "nets" in your life feel empty right now?

Where is Jesus inviting you to try again, even after failure?

What is one area of your life you can open to God's love this week?

How does your vocation or state of life become your mission field? In marriage, priesthood, religious life, or single life, these are the ways

---

[4] "Christ Has No Body," prayer traditionally attributed to St. Teresa of Ávila, but of uncertain authorship.

the Holy Spirit continuously guides us and leads us toward something greater: the ability to discover our true ontological destiny, journey toward our heavenly home, and help bring other souls there as well.

ACTION STEP: CASTING AGAIN WITH TRUST

This week, choose one area of your life in which it feels like you are "swimming upstream." Perhaps this is work stress, family conflict, prayer dryness, or financial worry.

Name It – Write it down in a journal or pray aloud: "Lord, here is where I feel stuck."

Surrender It – Place that situation symbolically at the foot of the Cross. You might do this by quietly tracing the Sign of the Cross over your heart or by lighting a candle before a crucifix at home or in the church.

Try Again at His Command – Ask Jesus for the courage to "try again" in this area, trusting His command (cf. Lk. 5:5): "Cast your net again." Resolve to take one small, concrete step of faith, making a call, forgiving someone, showing up to Mass, or setting aside time for prayer.

End with a Resounding Yes of Affirmation – Pray simply, "Yes, Lord, I trust You here."

Even a small "yes" invites strength into your struggle and turns exhaustion into grace.

Chapter Three

Hearts Transformed by Christ's Love

Image by the author, Eric Stengel.

A HEART CHECK

We all know the importance of heart health. We visit doctors, take medication, and watch our diet. But how often do we pause to check the health of our spiritual heart?

Every disciple carries wounds. Some are visible, such as broken relationships, illness, or loss. Others, like doubts, guilt, and shame, remain hidden. These wounds whisper the lie that we are unworthy of love. Yet Scripture tells us otherwise: "While we were still sinners, Christ died for us."[1] Jesus does not wait for perfection. He meets us in our brokenness, pouring His mercy into the very places where we hurt most.

Our healing begins where Jesus' Heart was opened for us. At Calvary, when the soldier pierced Jesus' side, blood and water flowed out (Jn 19:34). The Church Fathers saw symbolized in this the sacraments of baptism and Eucharist, the lifeblood of the Church. Christ's heart, pierced for love, is the wellspring of our healing. But His Sacred Heart is not only a symbol; it is a living Heart in which we see the reality that God's love is stronger than sin and death. In the piercing of that Heart, we see that, out of love for us, He will endure anything for our salvation. When we bring Him our wounds, He does not condemn us; He redeems us.

I remember sitting before the tabernacle one day, weighed down by shame. My eyes fell on the image of the Sacred Heart. In that moment, I realized His Heart is always open. My sins had not closed it; my doubts had not silenced it. Quietly, I laid down my burdens and trusted His mercy. I left lighter than when I arrived.

---

[1] Rom. 5:8

THE ETERNAL QUESTION

From the wounds of Christ's Heart, we turn to the question that shapes every heart: what do we live for, and where are we going? Do you believe your soul is eternal? Heaven, purgatory, and hell are not meant to frighten but to awaken us. Life is short; eternity is forever. Each Sunday, we profess in the Creed that our bodies will rise again. This truth changes everything. Every day becomes a gift from God, to Whom all souls will return to God one day.

In John 21, the disciples fished all night, but caught nothing until Jesus called from the shore, instructing them to cast their nets on the right side of the boat. Their obedience to this instruction led to an overflowing catch of 153 fish, none of which were lost. Our eternal destiny hinges on the same trust: will we cast our nets where He directs, or stubbornly persist in our own empty efforts?

ANOINTING OF THE SICK: CHRIST'S HEALING TOUCH

In times of illness or weakness, the Church reminds us that we are never alone. Through the sacrament of anointing of the sick, Christ comes as the Divine Physician, bringing peace, forgiveness, and often healing of body or soul.

I remember when my Grandma Evelyn received this sacrament. Though frail from a stroke, she carried a quiet strength. I believe that through Saint Joseph's intercession, the patron of a happy death, she passed peacefully and without regrets. Her sister was grateful that I had asked her parish priest to grant her this last sacrament. In the Letter of St. James, the apostle describes presbyters praying over and anointing the sick (Jas. 5:14-15). The anointing of the sick is the continuation of this practice today, in which the priest anoints the ailing person with the Oil of the Sick, olive oil that has been blessed by the Bishop of the Diocese. This sacrament is not only for the dying but for all facing serious illness or the frailty of age. It reminds us that even in suffering, Christ draws near, assuring us that no part of our lives falls outside His net of mercy.

I, too, have received this sacrament. It did not heal my sciatica, but it gave me the peace to be able to endure the pain. The gift is not always physical healing, but rather the courage and calm to keep rowing and casting alongside Christ.

FUNERALS AND THE FINAL COMMENDATION

When a loved one dies, the Church walks with us in our grief. Catholic funerals are not only moments to mourn but also profound acts of hope.

At the heart of the funeral liturgy is the Final Commendation, in which we entrust the soul of our brother or sister into the loving hands of God. In this prayer, the priest echoes Jesus' own words on the Cross: "Into your hands, Father of mercies, we commend our brother/sister."

Visiting a cemetery or columbarium to pray for deceased loved ones affirms that we remain bound together in the Communion of Saints. The net of Christ's love does not unravel at death; it gathers the Church triumphant, militant, and penitent into one vast catch destined for heaven.

THE LORD'S PRAYER: MORE THAN WORDS

Many of us rattle off the Our Father at Mass on autopilot. But this prayer is revolutionary. It is a cry for God's kingdom to break into our lives now, not just in some distant future.

"Thy will be done, on earth as it is in heaven." These words invite us to surrender our plans and align our lives with God's.

The Catechism teaches, "Man's vocation to eternal life does not suppress but actually reinforces his duty to put into action in this world the energies received from the Creator to serve justice and peace."[2]

Prayer, then, is not a checklist. It is a way of living in tune with God's heart.

WOUNDED HEARTS AND THE SACRED HEART

Each time we choose selfishness over love, it is like shooting an arrow into our own hearts and into the Heart of Christ. That is why devotion to the Sacred Heart is central to Catholic spirituality.

St. Augustine captured it well, saying, "Our hearts are restless until they rest in You."[3] That ache we feel is not a curse; it is a homing beacon drawing us back to God.

Peter denied Jesus three times, yet Jesus restored him by asking three times: "Do you love me?"[4] In the same way, the Sacrament of Reconciliation is where Christ repairs our brokenness and restores us to mission. Even if you have been away from Him for years, know that God never tires of forgiving.

---

[2] CCC 2820

[3] Augustine, *Confessions*, trans. Henry Chadwick (Oxford: Oxford University Press, 1991), 3 (I.1).

[4] Jn. 21:15-17

Sacred Heart of Jesus. Courtesy of Christine Barrantes

LOVE THAT COSTS SOMETHING

The Sacred Heart that loves also bleeds. Love that costs nothing remains shallow but love that suffers transforms. Today's culture treats love as a convenience. Yet Jesus shows us "agape" love, a sacrificial love that gives without counting the cost. Total trust and dependence on the Sacred Heart of Jesus remind us that the path of this life and the hope of the next are part of one journey, the journey toward union with God in Heaven. We are called to love and to be loved, both here on earth and in eternity, for that is the goal of every human heart.

Love that is real also costs something. It often involves suffering, sacrifice, and surrendering. Pope St John Paul II reminds us in his apostolic letter, *Salvifici Doloris*:

In bringing about the Redemption through suffering, Christ has also raised human suffering to the level of the Redemption.

Thus, each man, in his suffering, can also become a sharer in the redemptive suffering of Christ.[5]

In this mystery, we discover that true love and suffering are inseparable. When we unite our trials with the Cross of Christ, our pain becomes a prayer, our endurance becomes participation in His saving love, and our hearts are transformed into holy instruments of divine compassion.

When we unite our pain to His Cross, our struggles are not wasted. They become part of the great catch, our small offerings woven into Christ's redemptive net for the world.

THE DAILY EXAMEN: A PRACTICAL TOOL

The Ignatian practice of the Daily Examen offers a simple yet profound way to reflect on God's presence in our daily lives and keep our love for God and neighbor alive:

- Give Thanks – Begin by reflecting on the blessings you received throughout the day. Consider how you have shown gratitude for these gifts and take a moment to thank God for His abundant grace.

- Ask for Light – Invite God to open your heart and mind, helping you become more aware of His presence in your daily activities, whether at work, school, or during leisure.

- Review the Day – Reflect on your day with an open mind. Identify moments of consolation in which God's presence was evident through your actions and encounters. Also acknowledge

---

[5] John Paul II, On the Christian Meaning of Human Suffering *Salvifici Doloris* (11 February 1984) §19, at the Holy See, https://www.vatican.va/content/john-paul-ii/en/apost_letters/1984/documents/hf_jp-ii_apl_11021984_salvifici-doloris.html.

moments of desolation, where your choices may have distanced you from Him.

- Seek Forgiveness – Humbly ask for God's mercy for the times you fell short of His will. Reflect on the opportunities you've missed to live out the Gospel and share His love with others.
- Resolution to Change – Make a conscious commitment to better align your life with God's love and will. Consider specific ways to improve your attitude, behavior, and responses in the days ahead.[6]

My late grandmother Doris often ended her letters with the words, "In love and light." That is the Christian life. When our love for Jesus flourishes, we become light for others. To live "in love and light" is to dwell in the Heart of Jesus. It is there that our wounds find healing, our fears find peace, and our love finds purpose.

REFLECTION QUESTIONS
FROM CHAPTER THREE

Is my heart restless, or is it resting in God?

What wounds do I have that need healing today?

---

[6] The Jesuit Institute, "What is the Examen", Retrieved from https://jesuitinstitute.org/Pages/Examen.htm, accessed on January 14, 2024.

When have I experienced Christ's healing presence in times of weakness or suffering? This can be through prayer, the sacraments, or the love of others.

How does visiting a cemetery, praying at a columbarium, or recalling the Final Commendation at a funeral help open my heart to God's love and deepen my trust in His promise of eternal life?

Am I willing to let God's love "shoot through" my heart not to wound, but to heal?

Chapter Four

Casting Nets,
Sharing Catches

Feeding of the Thousands, fresco in Hagia Sophia, Trabzon.
Public domain.

SMALL ACTS, BIG IMPACT

One of my earliest memories of performing an act of kindness occurred when I was in first grade. A classmate's art project blew away in the wind, and I chased it down for her. It seemed like a small thing at the time, but her gratitude stayed with me. That moment planted a seed: even little acts matter.

Later, while serving as a Eucharistic minister, I brought Communion to the sick and elderly. I will never forget one man named Mike, who was recovering from a heart attack. As he received the Eucharist, peace came over his face. Christ Himself was present, bringing healing and hope. Mike and his wife, Jeanie, later started a ministry at our church, the Mother Teresa Ministry, to bring Holy Communion to those in the hospital.

These moments taught me that discipleship is often about small nets, not big catches. Not everyone is meant for heroic deeds, but all are intended to practice love every day.

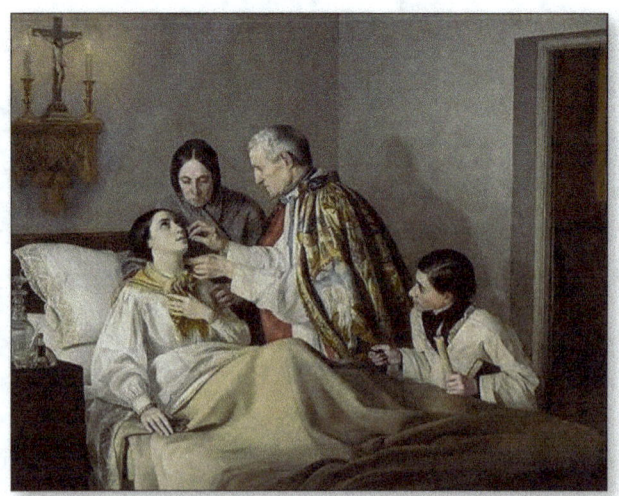

*Viaticum, Tadeusz Gorecki, 1852, National
Museum, Warsaw. Public domain.*

PSALM 139: KNOWN AND LOVED BY GOD

Psalm 139 reminds us that God has always known us: "You formed my inmost being you knit me in my mother's womb."[1]

This is a reminder that your life is not random. Even if you doubt your worth, God had a plan for you before you were born. This psalm affirms the Church's teaching on human dignity, which states that every person is created in God's image and entrusted with a mission.

You are not an accident. You are God's beloved.

My friend Peter Cao once wrote beautifully about learning to receive from God and live generously. His story shows that discipleship is not just about what we give, but how we open ourselves to the Holy Spirit and allow God to act in us. With his permission, I share his story here:

LEARNING THE ART OF RECEIVING AND BEING RESPONSIVE

Fr. Jacques Philippe once wrote:

It is vitally important to learn to receive, to receive one's very own self along with everything from God. To the extent we learn to receive everything from God, we can give to others the best of ourselves.[2]

As Christians, we are called to sacrifice as Christ did, giving of ourselves generously. Yet as Saint Thérèse of Lisieux reminds us,

---

[1] Ps. 139:13
[2] Jacques Philippe, *Fire & Light: Learning to Receive the Gift of God* (New York: Scepter Publishers, 2016).

"The merit doesn't consist in doing or in giving a lot, but rather in receiving, in loving a lot."[3]

PETER REFLECTS

Growing up as a perfectionist, Peter tied his self-worth to productivity. Giving came naturally, but receiving felt foreign. Rediscovering the value of relationships taught him the humility of receiving. It showed him that we thrive only with the support of others and the gifts of the Holy Spirit.

BEING OPEN TO THE HOLY SPIRIT

Raised as a cradle Catholic, Peter's early prayers were rote. In adulthood, a professional crisis reignited his faith and drew him into the charismatic Sword of the Spirit movement. At first, the enthusiastic worship unsettled him, but slowly, the Holy Spirit reshaped his heart.

He learned to call on the Spirit before teaching baptism classes, meeting patients, or speaking with brothers in his faith community. This openness allowed him to overcome social anxiety and gave him the courage to share his faith.

Peter recalls the witness of Fr. Walter Ciszek, who survived twenty-three years in Soviet prisons:

> *God in His providence must make use of our tragedies to remind our fallen human nature of His presence and love... The failing is on our part. He is always present and ever faithful.*[4]

---

[3] St. Thérèse of Lisieux, *Letter 142 to Céline* (July 26, 1893), in *Letters of St. Thérèse of Lisieux*, Vol. 2, ICS Publications.

[4] Walter Ciszek, *He Leadeth Me: An Extraordinary Testament of Faith* (New York: Image, 2014).

Like Fr. Ciszek, Peter discovered that true faith means trusting God in hardship and asking the Spirit for strength daily. Even in trivial things like asking friends to help take down Christmas lights, he learned that openness to others and to God allows us to become holy gifts for the world.

This openness echoes the call to ongoing conversion and surrender to divine providence. It is a reminder that prayer does not have to be perfect; it simply needs to be open and honest.

EMBRACING LEISURE

Peter also admits he struggled with rest. On vacations, his drive for productivity took over, like on his honeymoon in Barcelona, during which he dragged his exhausted wife on a late-night subway ride to see a Gaudí building.

He later realized, as Dr. Michael Naughton writes, "When we take by force those things that should only be received, we violate the divine image within us."[5]

Through silence, Sabbath, and feasting, Peter discovered that true leisure is a form of receptivity. He practiced this during the Exodus 90 program, in which he found that even fifteen minutes of silent prayer proved challenging yet life giving. In the Catholic life, silence becomes a space where the heart can finally hear God, free from noise, distraction, and the constant pull of productivity. Sabbath invites us to rest in God by setting aside ordinary work, making space for worship, renewal, and the simple joy of being rather than doing. Feasting, which follows seasons of fasting or discipline,

---

[5] Michael Naughton, *Getting Work Right: Labor and Leisure in a Fragmented World* (Steubenville: Emmaus Road Publishing, 2019).

reminds us that God also delights in our joy, expressed through shared meals, celebration, community, and gratitude for the gifts He gives. Together, these practices form a rhythm that helps us receive rather than grasp, allowing grace to shape our days in ways we could never cultivate on our own.

As Cardinal Robert Sarah notes, "Our world no longer hears God because it is constantly speaking... to say nothing."[6]

GENEROSITY AS A RESPONSE

Receiving leads to generosity. Mother Teresa exemplified this in her life. As she said, "I must be willing to give whatever it takes to do good to others. This requires that I be willing to give until it hurts. Otherwise, there is no true love in me."[7]

Cao Family Saint Joseph Altar for the Dedication to Saint Joseph Feast Day. Photo by Peter Cao.

---

[6] Robert Sarah, *The Power of Silence: Against the Dictatorship of Noise* (San Francisco: Ignatius Press, 2017)

[7] Mother Teresa, *In the Heart of the World: Thoughts, Prayers, and Stories* (New York: MJF Books, 2002)

Peter reflects that marriage and fatherhood challenged his tendency to hoard. Slowly, he learned to share love, time, and resources as gifts from God. St. Thérèse's Little Way showed him that even small encouragements such as a kind word or a simple act could build God's Kingdom.

YEAR OF SAINT JOSEPH

In 2021, Peter consecrated himself to St. Joseph during the Year of St. Joseph, which had been proclaimed by Pope Francis. He quotes Fr. Donald Calloway, who said, "The greatness of St. Joseph is that he was willing to become a homeless wanderer out of love for God and Mary."[8]

For Peter, Joseph became a model of humility, quiet service, and devotion, a reminder that holiness often looks like silent, steadfast love.

DRAWING THE NET TOGETHER

Saint Thérèse of Lisieux called the finding of holiness in ordinary acts of love the "Little Way." She said, "Without love, deeds, even the most brilliant, count as nothing."[9] Her words remind us that God sees not only what we do but also the love with which we do it.

The Eucharist strengthens us for this daily mission. Each Mass is a sending forth to live the Gospel at home, at work, and at school. The Paschal Mystery is made present not only on the altar but also in our lives when we bear one another's burdens, as St. Paul tells us

---

[8] Donald Calloway, *Consecration to St. Joseph: The Wonders of Our Spiritual Father* (Stockbridge: Marian Press, 2020).
[9] Thérèse of Lisieux, *Story of a Soul: The Autobiography of St. Thérèse of Lisieux*, trans. John Beevers (Notre Dame, IN: Ave Maria Press, 1996), [page number].

in his letter to the Galatians: "Bear one another's burdens, and so fulfill the law of Christ."[10]

The visible example of our witness is required. The world is more hungry for compassion than arguments. Showing Christ's love through kindness, forgiveness, and mercy directs others to Him, rather than to ourselves.

REFLECTION QUESTIONS FROM CHAPTER FOUR

Do you find it easier to give or to receive? Why?

Where might the Holy Spirit be nudging you to open your heart more fully?

What small act of generosity could you offer this week?

How can you practice Sabbath or true rest so your discipleship in Christ remains strong?

---

[10] Gal. 6:2

How does St. Joseph's humility inspire you in your family or daily work?

ACTION STEP: LIVING THE LITTLE WAY

Return – Recenter your week on the Eucharist. If possible, attend one weekday Mass or spend ten minutes in silent prayer before the tabernacle, offering your ordinary life to God.

Renew – Choose one daily activity such as work, cooking, errands, or family care, and intentionally offer it to

God as prayer. Remind yourself that even the smallest acts can glorify Him.

Reach Out – Perform one hidden act of kindness for someone: write a note, wash a dish without being asked, or encourage a co-worker. Do it quietly, without seeking recognition.

Pray Simply – End your day with St. Thérèse's prayer:

Jesus, I will seek out a means of getting to heaven by a little way very short and very straight, a little way that is wholly new.[11]

---

[11] Thérèse of Lisieux, *Story of a Soul: The Autobiography of St. Thérèse of Lisieux*, trans. John Clarke, O.C.D., 3rd ed. (Washington, DC: ICS Publications, 1996), 207.

Chapter Five

Living in God's Gaze

Salmon West of Destruction, David M. Waller.
Photo by Eric Stengel.

WATCHFULNESS IN THE WATERS

Every fisherman knows the importance of watchfulness. Watching the waters for signs of life is as important as lowering the nets. To live in God's gaze is to cast faithfully, knowing His watchful eye is always upon us.

JACK'S STORY

My late grandfather, Jack, was an award-winning photographer, whose work was displayed at art exhibits across the United States. His passion began with pinhole and Argus cameras that he carried during World War II, in which he served as an infantry soldier. Though he rarely spoke of the war, his photos revealed life's beauty and resilience, even in hardship.

During the war, his dog tag saved his life, coming between him and a bullet from the enemy. After that, his faith grew deeper. I remember him carrying a missal (daily readings from the Bible) to Mass and keeping a well-worn copy of his Holy Bible close at hand (see chapter 10). These were signs of a faith that shaped our family.

One treasured heirloom in our family is a painting gifted to Jack by artist David M. Waller, titled Salmon West of Destruction. Its light glows in our home today, reminding me of Christ, the true Light of the World (Jn. 1:5).

REFLECTION

How can I use my own gifts, talents, or passions as Jack did with photography to reflect God's light and bear witness to His presence in the world?

GERALD AND EVELYN

My paternal grandparents, Gerald and Evelyn, were also people of deep faith. Gerald, a veteran of the United States Army Air Corps who later became a teacher, faced his ultimate battle with cancer with remarkable peace and a confident readiness for eternal life. Evelyn's steadfast devotion to prayer sustained her through many trials and bore witness to her trust in God's providence. Having lost her parents in a car crash as a young adult and needing to take on the responsibility of caring for her younger brother and two sisters, she knew adversity well.

Together, Gerald and Evelyn's life reflected the call of Christ to cast the net in faith. Like Saint Paul, they could say, "I have fought the good fight, I have finished the race, I have kept the faith."[1] Even in suffering, they remained within the unbroken net of Christ's love, a reminder that every generation is gathered and held secure in His mercy.

Gerald passed away when I was less than two years old. I grew up hearing stories about his quiet witness and vocation. After the war, he worked multiple jobs as a civilian aircraft mechanic at various Texas bases, but his favorite role was teaching small engine repair to eager students. Cancer and surgical complications ended his life too soon, but God's grace was evident in his final days. In an audio interview recorded while in hospice, Gerald spoke with courage and unwavering trust in Christ with no hint of regret. Even in suffering, he remained a steadfast defender of the faith.

---

[1] 2 Tim. 4:7

REFLECTION

How does the example of Gerald and Evelyn encourage me to remain faithful in times of trial and to trust that God holds each generation in the net of His love?

EVELYN'S BARN FIRE

My father often tells a story from his youth that leaves a deep impression on others, including myself. One day, a fire broke out in the family dairy barn. Flames could be seen from miles away in their small agrarian community. With no large fire department, neighbors rushed from surrounding farms to help.

During the panic, my grandmother Evelyn paused, prayed, and grabbed a small container of holy water to sprinkle toward the barn fire. Her neighbors, who were not Catholic, thought she was out of her mind. My dad remembers them saying, "Lady, that is not going to put out the fire," as they continued to throw pails of water on the blaze.

The fire destroyed the dairy barn. Yet, as my father recalls, the wind suddenly stopped after my grandmother prayed and sprinkled the holy water, sparing the nearby house. He has always seen it as a miracle that their home was saved.

Sacramentals such as crucifixes, medals, rosaries, and holy water serve as visible signs of God's grace and presence. They help us grow in holiness by reminding us to turn our hearts toward Christ. Sacramentals are not magic; they are powerful because they are rooted in prayer and the blessing of the Church.

My grandmother's faith shows how sacramentals can anchor us in moments of crisis. The holy water she used did not put out the flames, but it lifted her family's gaze toward God and renewed their trust in His providence.

REFLECTION

How do sacramentals in my life, such as holy water or the rosary, help me turn my heart toward God and trust in His care during moments of trial?

ANDREW'S STORY

The fact that my brother Andrew, who was born with spina bifida, walks today, by God's grace, is a miracle akin to the apostles pulling in an unexpected catch. His condition was so severe that doctors said he was only centimeters away from life in a wheelchair.

In those anxious early days, my mother leaned quietly on the faith handed down by her mother and grandmother. They urged her to pray and to bless Andrew with holy water brought from Lourdes in France, where the Blessed Virgin Mary appeared to Saint Bernadette. For generations, pilgrims have journeyed to Lourdes seeking healing at the spring that flows near the grotto. With simple and trusting faith, my mother sprinkled the water over Andrew and placed his life in God's hands.

I remember my father leading our family in the rosary during long hospital stays and the many surgeries my brother endured. The steady rhythm of those prayers remains with me, a memory I now carry into the life of my own family. As the late Father Patrick Peyton once said, "The family that prays together stays together." In the midst of fear and uncertainty, prayer and God's grace became the quiet strength that held our family together during that difficult season.

Though the outcome could have been very different, Andrew grew strong. He learned to walk and continues to do so today, a living reminder of the quiet ways God works. His story is not only about survival but about God's providence woven into the ordinary faith of mothers and grandmothers who believed in prayer.

Andrew's journey reminds us that God still fills our nets in ways we cannot predict. Just as the disciples once found their nets overflowing after a night of failure, we, too, discover that God surprises us with blessings beyond what we could imagine.

REFLECTION

Where has God surprised me with blessings I did not expect, and how can I respond with gratitude and trust like my family did in Andrew's story?

Not every miracle makes headlines or dramatically defies the laws of nature. Many are quiet, almost hidden like a house spared from fire or a child given strength to walk. These small miracles remind us that God is present not only in extraordinary signs but also in the ordinary moments when faith meets trust.

Faith is often more caught than taught. The lived witness of family, neighbors, and friends becomes the lens through which we notice God's presence in daily life. Their examples of prayer, trust, and perseverance help us recognize that God may be working quietly in our own story, too.

REFLECTION

Where has God's providence protected me, sustained me, or surprised me in ways I might otherwise have overlooked?

PRAYER: THE HEART OF DISCIPLESHIP

Prayer roots us in this gaze of God. Saint Thérèse of Lisieux described it beautifully, "For me, prayer is a surge of the heart; it is a simple look turned toward heaven, a cry of recognition and love."[2]

Pope Francis, in his preparation for the 2025 Jubilee Year, reminded us that prayer is "the royal road to holiness,"[3] encouraging us to make the Our Father a life program of discipleship.

But what is prayer? The Catechism defines it as "the raising of one's mind and heart to God."[4] Prayer is both personal and communal. It engages us fully and calls us to live intentionally, returning to Christ even when we falter.

John Michael Talbot, a Franciscan hermit and composer, reflects on this depth in his work *The Lover and the Beloved*, saying,

> *"Contemplation of God's being and oneness elevates the soul into divine wonder. God is alive! God is infinite!"*[5]

Prayer, at its best, leads us into this encounter with the living God.

REFLECTION

How do I let prayer shape not only my words, but the way I live each day as a disciple?

---

[2] St. Thérèse of Lisieux, *Story of a Soul*, trans. John Clarke, 3rd ed. (Washington, DC: ICS Publications, 1996), 242.

[3] Pope Francis, A Year of Preparation for the Jubilee 2025: Prayer, Vatican (2024), 5.

[4] Catechism of the Catholic Church, 2nd ed. (Vatican City: Libreria Editrice Vaticana, 1997), §2559.

[5] John Michael Talbot, *The Lover and the Beloved* (San Francisco: HarperSanFrancisco, 1986), 46.

MYSTICAL ENCOUNTERS WITH GOD

Prayer is not just words, but an encounter. Sometimes God stirs our hearts in unexpected ways. I was eight years old when my grandmother, Thecia, passed away. That night, I awoke to storms followed by gentle rain. Though filled with grief, I suddenly experienced a deep peace, a mysterious joy that I now recognize as God's presence.

I remember Thecia as an avid bowler, and that night the crack of lightning felt to me like the sound of a bowling strike. As the storm gave way to the gentle calm of rain, I learned the news of her passing, and our family went together to comfort my grandfather, Jack. In my young heart, I thought, she hit a strike in heaven for sure.

Such moments remind us that even in loss, God gives signs of His closeness. Prayer opens us to recognize these gifts, teaching us that love endures beyond death and that His presence is never absent.

REFLECTION

Have I ever experienced a moment of unexpected peace or a small sign of God's closeness during loss or sorrow?

The Angelus, Jean-François Millet, 1857–1859.
Public domain. "Teach us how to pray."

TEACH US HOW TO PRAY

French artist Jean-François Millet's painting *The Angelus* depicts two humble farmers pausing from their work to pray at the sound of church bells. This scene of prayerful simplicity reflects Mary's fiat and reminds us that holiness begins in daily moments.

Jesus teaches us how to pray, saying, "When you pray, say, Our Father..."[6] The Our Father draws us into God's presence, teaches forgiveness, and centers us in His providence. In times of worry, repeating its words restores peace.

OVERCOMING THE NOISE

In a world of constant noise, technology, and division, prayer is countercultural. It quiets the soul and draws us back to the essentials. Just as Jesus refocused His disciples amid Roman and religious strife, so too He invites us to silence distractions and rediscover God's voice.

True prayer is not an escape from our problems but a transformation of our entire being. It opens us to God's love, unites us to the Church, and equips us to live as witnesses of hope.

THE UNIFYING GUIDE

In Matthew's Gospel, Jesus offers us the Our Father, a prayer that encapsulates His core teachings. It serves as a unifying guide to center us on God's will, cutting through the noise of division and confusion:

Our Father in heaven, Hallowed be your name,
Your kingdom come, Your will be done,
On earth as in heaven.

---

[6] Mt. 6:9

49

Give us today our daily bread; And forgive us our debts,
As we forgive our debtors;
and do not subject us to the final test,
But deliver us from the evil one.[7]

This prayer calls us to unity, humility, and trust in God's providence, reminding us to set aside divisions and focus on the path Jesus has shown us.

The Catechism of the Catholic Church beautifully explains the Our Father's connection to the Kingdom of God:

It is brought near in the Word incarnate, it is proclaimed throughout the whole Gospel, and it has come in Christ's death and Resurrection. The Kingdom of God has been coming since the Last Supper and, in the Eucharist, it is in our midst. The Kingdom will come in glory when Christ hands it over to His Father.[8]

This teaching reminds us that the Kingdom of God is both present and yet to come, made manifest through Christ's Incarnation, His sacrificial death, and His Resurrection. In the Eucharist, we experience the Kingdom in our midst while also anticipating its ultimate fulfillment.

The Our Father is more than a prayer; it is a call to daily live the truths it professes. It invites us to surrender to God's will, trust in His providence, and unite as His children. Amid division and noise, it centers us on the Gospel, reminding us that the Kingdom of God is both present and yet to come. Through Christ's presence, especially

---

[7] Mt. 6:9–13
[8] CCC 2816.

in the Eucharist, we experience this Kingdom and are called to be its instruments, bringing unity, forgiveness, and love to a world longing for peace.

REFLECTION

How can praying the Our Father each day help me surrender distractions and trust more fully in God's providence?

PRAYER IN DAILY LIFE

Prayer is both communal and personal. In the Eucharist and the Liturgy of the Hours, we unite with the whole Church. In personal prayer, whether the rosary, Scripture, or heartfelt words, we meet God in intimacy. Both sustain us, reminding us that prayer is not only what we say but how we live. Every action, thought, and choice can be a way of honoring God when it is done with love and faith.

Every day, Jesus asks us the same question He asked Peter, "Do you love me?" Our answer is shown not only in our prayers but also in how we care for others and serve those in need, following His example.

By combining both communal and personal prayer, we grow closer to God and to one another. The prayers of the Church give us strength and direction, while private prayer brings peace and a deeper connection to God. Together, they guide us to live faithfully by dedicating each moment to loving and honoring Him.

LIVING IN GOD'S GAZE: A CLOSING WORD

The stories of Jack, Thecia, Gerald, and Evelyn, the barn fire, and Andrew's miracle of walking all testify that God's gaze remains constant and His love unbroken. Whether through sacramentals, prayer, family traditions, or unexpected moments of grace, He draws us back to Himself repeatedly.

To live in God's gaze is to trust that nothing is wasted, not suffering, not loss, not even the smallest act of faith. Each becomes a stitch in the fabric of His providence, a thread in the unbroken net of Christ's love.

As we journey along the narrow but challenging road of life each day, may we remember that God is watching with love, ready to surprise us with blessings, strengthen us through trials, and hold us together as one family in the Body of Christ.

Will we fix our gaze upon Jesus' outstretched hand, trusting that He points us toward the right path so that we may bear abundant and lasting grace?

REFLECTION QUESTIONS FROM CHAPTER FIVE

How can I use my own gifts, talents, or passions as Jack did with photography to reflect God's light and bear witness to His presence in the world?

How does the example of Gerald and Evelyn encourage me to remain faithful in times of trial and to trust that God holds each generation in the net of His love?

How do sacramentals, such as holy water or the rosary, help me turn my heart toward God and trust in His care during moments of trial?

Where has God surprised me with blessings I did not expect, and how can I respond with gratitude and trust like my family did in Andrew's story?

How does remembering my Baptism or the Baptism of a loved one help me see that I am woven into God's family and securely held in the unbroken net of His love?

How do I let prayer shape not only my words but also the way I live each day as a disciple?

Have I ever experienced a moment of unexpected peace or a small sign of God's nearness during loss or sorrow?

How can praying the Our Father each day help me surrender distractions and trust more fully in God's providence?

What simple prayer practice could I begin or strengthen with my family, friends, or community to draw us closer to God and one another?

ACTION STEP: LIVING A PRAYER-FILLED LIFE

Return – Commit this week to praying the Our Father slowly and intentionally once each day. Let each line guide your heart back to God's will.

Renew – Choose one daily activity, such as commuting, cooking, or walking, and transform it into a moment of prayer by quietly inviting the Holy Spirit into that space.

Reach Out – Ask someone in your family, parish, or workplace if you can pray for them. Even a simple promise, *"I'll keep you in prayer,"* can open hearts to God's love.

Pray Simply – End each day with a humble prayer of St. Thérèse, who said, "For me, prayer is a surge of the heart; it is a simple look turned toward heaven, a cry of recognition and love."

Notice, Pray, and Share – Ask a parent, grandparent, or elder in your parish to share a moment when they experienced God's providence. Reflect on your own life: where have you seen quiet miracles of His care? Bring these memories into prayer, thanking God for His presence in small and hidden ways. Then share your story with someone else, allowing faith to be "caught" through your witness.

Chapter Six

Marriage and Vocation:
A Shared Path of Prayer

Eric & Angela's Sacrament of Matrimony,
wedding photo at Saint Joseph Church

DISCOVERING VOCATION IN SINGLENESS

When I was single and walking with the Lord, I didn't realize that singleness is a vocation with dignity and purpose. Living chastely and walking humbly with Christ wasn't meant to be a waiting room for another calling, but a mission field where God was already forming my heart and using my life.

As the prophet Micah asks, "What does the Lord require of you but to do justice, and to love kindness, and to walk humbly with your God?"[1] This is a mission that can and should be pursued in every stage of life, including the time of singleness.

Discernment is an important part of this mission. In an early season of my life, I was trying to understand where God was leading me and how best to offer my life in love. I did not always know what the future would hold, but I could see that Christ was gently guiding my steps. Just as Jesus asked the disciples to cast their nets on the right side of the boat, I sensed the Holy Spirit inviting me to trust again, to cast my heart into the deep, believing that I would one day share in the covenant of selfless love that is the sacred bond of marriage.

The vocation of love was not denied to me in times of uncertainty or transition. It was graciously redirected. For years, I lived in the vocation of singleness. Those years were not wasted. They became a covenant with God, a time of learning to show the love of Christ to others through friendship, service, and acts of compassion. Singleness was not a holding space. It was a real calling to reveal the tenderness of Christ in ordinary life and daily relationships.

---

[1] Mic. 6:8

Only later, in a time I could not have predicted, I met Angela and began to see how God had been preparing both of us for a life together. The covenant of marriage became the next chapter in that story of love, shaped by the grace that had already formed me in the years before.

This calling to the covenant of love asks for a daily offering of oneself, a patient carrying of one another's burdens, and a desire to show the presence of Christ through simple and generous love. It is not only a gift we receive, but a way of life we are invited to live with tenderness and trust.

MEETING ANGELA AND THE CALL TO MATRIMONY

In God's providence, I eventually met Angela. Though we had grown up in the same parish, our paths only crossed for the first time when we connected through a Catholic dating site. What seemed like a coincidence was truly God's timing.

After nearly two years of friendship, prayer, and discernment, we embraced matrimony, the sacrament in which God Himself consecrates the covenant of husband and wife as a living sign of Christ's love for His Church (cf. Eph. 5:25–32).

Marriage is not merely a human contract; it is a covenant that mirrors God's unbreakable bond with His people. In this covenant, the gift of children becomes a visible sign of God's life-giving love: "Be fruitful and multiply and fill the earth."[2]

---

[2] Gen. 1:28

DAILY FIDELITY IN FAMILY LIFE

Through the years, both joyful and challenging, I have discovered that marriage calls me to die to myself daily. Unlike the single life, in which I was freer to choose when and how to serve, my vocation as husband and father requires me to resemble Christ for my wife and daughter every day.

Jesus' words to Peter challenge me daily: "Do you love me? ... Feed my sheep."[3]

Without God's grace, our family would drift like a ship without the North Star. But with Christ as our star, prayer as our compass, and the sacraments as our sails, our family can plot a steady course. Our home becomes "a domestic church"[4] woven together in love, faith, and sacrifice.

A LIVING TESTIMONY OF PRAYER: ANGELA'S STORY

Angela's story reminds me of the truth proclaimed by Jesus, "Where two or three are gathered in my name, there am I in the midst of them."[5] From courtship through marriage and into family life, prayer has been the thread weaving our lives together into one life of love. I'll let her share her side of the story in her own words:

When I met Eric, I was overjoyed to find someone who shared my Catholic faith. We started spending time together as friends. We

---

[3] Jn. 21:15-17

[4] Second Vatican Council, *Dogmatic Constitution on the Church: Lumen Gentium*, §11, Vatican.va, https://www.vatican.va/archive/hist_councils/ii_vatican_council/documents/vat-ii_const_19641121_lumen-gentium_en.html.

[5] Mt. 18:20

enjoyed fun activities like going to dinner, bowling, dancing, and taking long walks, getting to know each other.

One of my favorite memories together is my 30th birthday, when Eric joined me in fulfilling one of my bucket list items. I had always wanted to walk all the way around White Rock Lake in Dallas, which is 9.4 miles around. We made it the full distance and didn't run out of conversation, which was a great sign that we were a good match for one another.

Though we had grown up in the same parish, we had never crossed paths until we met on that Catholic dating site. I had come to realize how important it was to me to spend time with someone who shared my faith. One evening, I found myself searching for "Catholic dating," and the rest was history.

I had always considered attending various young adult activities, but I was too timid to go alone. Once I met Eric, we started going together. Every Monday night, we met with a group of young adults for praise and worship, discussion, Liturgy of the Hours, and Eucharistic Adoration, followed by fellowship. Monday nights quickly became one of my favorite parts of the week.

Though we met many friends along the way, it was the two of us who were growing together in our faith, ultimately leading our friendship to blossom into a loving relationship. A year after dating, Eric surprised me with a picnic at White Rock Lake, where he asked me to be his wife. We married a year later and were blessed with our sweet daughter, Abigail.

Prayer remains a regular part of our family routine. Eric and I will sometimes start our day together with the Liturgy of the Hours before our morning coffee. This is a quiet time of reflection for both of us before we begin the day. We also say family rosaries with

Abby and participate in various faith-building activities through our parish.

These moments in prayer bring us closer as a family, ultimately leading each other to a life filled with faith, love, and joy.

MARRIAGE AS VOCATION

The Catechism of the Catholic Church reminds us that marriage is "ordered to the good of the spouses and the procreation and education of offspring."[6] It is not simply a natural bond but a sacrament instituted by Christ.

PRAYER AS COVENANT LIFE

Family prayer strengthens the domestic church, making Christ present in the home. By praying together, the family participates in the mission of the universal Church, drawing grace into daily life.

THE FAMILY AS DOMESTIC CHURCH

Just as the disciples in the early Church met in their homes for "the breaking of the bread and the prayers,"[7] so too the Christian household is meant to be a place where faith is lived, taught, and celebrated.

REFLECTION QUESTIONS
FROM CHAPTER SIX

How did you first come to understand your vocation in life?

---

[6] CCC 1601
[7] Acts 2:42

How has that understanding changed over time?

What role does prayer play in your family or closest relationships?

In what ways does marriage (or family life) challenge you to live less for yourself and more for Christ and others?

How can your "domestic church" become more visibly a place of faith, prayer, and service?

ACTION STEPS

Notice – Pay attention this week to the patterns in your family life. Are they shaped by prayer, trust, and love or by busyness and distraction?

Pray – Commit to one shared family prayer time each day (for example, grace before meals, a decade of the Rosary, or a morning offering).

Share – Talk with your spouse, child, or a close friend about how you can support one another in faith. Make a plan to attend Mass or parish prayer together this week.

CLOSING PRAYER

Heavenly Father,

You call us to walk faithfully in the vocation of love.

Bless our families, that our homes may become true domestic churches.

Grant us the grace to love selflessly, as Christ loves His Church. May our prayer be the bond that unites us, our faith the anchor that secures us in trials, and our hope the light that guides us toward heaven.

Through the intercession of the Holy Family of Nazareth, guide us in our vocation of love.

We ask this through Christ our Lord. Amen.

Eric teaching his young daughter, Abigail, the importance of prayer. Photo by Angela Stengel.

Chapter Seven

A School of Fish

Image by Angela Stengel

THE SIGN OF THE FISH

The early Christians chose the fish as their cryptic sign, a mark of belonging in a world where martyrdom for the faith was a stark reality. In the early centuries, when believers faced persecution under Roman authority, Christians would draw the simple outline of a fish in the dirt or on a stone as a discreet way of identifying one another.

The Greek word Ichthus, an acronym for Iēsous Christos Theou Huios Sōtēr ("Jesus Christ, Son of God, Savior"), carried both theological depth and communal identity. For those early disciples, it was not just a secret sign of belonging but a confession of faith in the One who called them to be "fishers of men."[1]

This simple symbol still speaks profoundly today. A lone fish may drift aimlessly, but a school of fish moves with unity and purpose. We are not meant merely to exist alongside one another in faith but to live in communion, guided by the Spirit, as one Body of Christ.

KNOTS ON THE NET: THE SACRAMENTS

Just as knots hold together the strands of a net, the sacraments bind us together as the People of God. Baptism brings us into the Church, Confirmation strengthens us with the Spirit, and the Eucharist nourishes us with the Body and Blood of Christ. Each sacrament is a gift of grace that secures us within Christ's unbreakable net of love.

I remember when Angela and I gave the gift of a baptismal box to our goddaughter. It was a small but meaningful sign that her life had been caught up into something greater than herself, anchored in the grace of Baptism. At Baptism, we are anointed with the oil of

---

[1] Mk 1:17

chrism, marked forever as God's children, and called to share in the threefold mission of Christ as priest, prophet, and king. The Spirit strengthens us to live this mission daily in prayer, witness, and service.

THE SACRAMENTS ANCHOR US IN UNITY

The sacraments anchor us in unity. In Baptism, we are immersed in the life of Christ and reborn as new creations in His Body. Confirmation seals us with the Holy Spirit and empowers us with His seven gifts to live as mature disciples. In the Eucharist, we are nourished by His very Body and strengthened to love one another through the power of His grace and His eternal, abundant love for all creation.

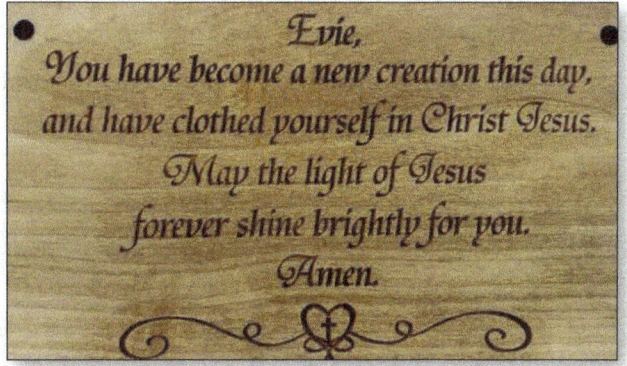

Engraving from the Baptismal Keepsake Box:
a reminder that in baptism we are sealed with
Christ and marked forever as God's children.

THE QUILT OF BAPTISM

At my niece's baptism on December 20, her parents—my sister and her husband—received a quilt for her that was passed down from my great-grandmother. This gift was more than fabric and thread; it carried the prayers, faith, and love of generations.

Just as the waters of Baptism weave us into the Body of Christ, the quilt became a visible reminder of the faith and family into which she was now more deeply bound.

Angela, who providentially shares the same baptismal date (or baptismal birthday as we call it) as our niece and goddaughter, also has a love for quilting that continues the tradition of my great-grandparents. For her, quilting is more than a craft; it is a way of stitching together memories, stories, and love into something lasting.

In this, her art mirrors the grace of Baptism, in which God weaves us into the fabric of His Church. Just as each patch and thread contributes to the beauty of a quilt, so too each soul, bound by the waters of Baptism, strengthens the unbroken net of Christ's love that gathers us into one Body, the Church.

How does remembering my Baptism anniversary, or the Baptism of a loved one, help me see that I am woven into God's family and securely held in the unbroken net of His love?

Cherished Family Heirloom, serving as a
reminder of God's Love in the World

THE SACRAMENT OF BAPTISM

The Sacrament of Baptism is the first sacrament of initiation that grounds us in Christ, through which we become children of the light and are made new creations. My own baptismal birthday, March 23, was one month after my physical birth on February 23. This is a profound coincidence for me and for others within the fabric of time that shapes our spiritual journey, a gentle reminder that the Lord provides us with signs and wonders if only we take the time to look up and notice them. When is your baptismal birthday?

CONFIRMATION:
SEALED WITH THE SPIRIT

After Sacrament of Baptism, Reconciliation and Holy Communion, the sacrament I recall most vividly is Confirmation. Bishop Charles anointed my forehead with sacred chrism, declaring, "Be sealed with the gift of the Holy Spirit." The fragrance of the oil lingered as a sign that God's mark is not fleeting but permanent. That same sacred chrism was first poured over me in Baptism, when I was claimed for Christ and called to live as priest, prophet, and king. At Confirmation, the seal was renewed and strengthened, reminding me that I am not my own; I belong to God.

My teacher, Harold, helped me understand that this sacrament was not a graduation from religious education but the beginning of a deeper call. It was my personal Pentecost, a moment when the Spirit was poured out anew, not as tongues of fire but as an inner courage to live the Gospel. Just as the apostles left the Upper Room aflame with zeal, so too Confirmation sends us forth to bring the light of Christ into a world in need.

When I think back to that day, I realize that God's Spirit was inviting me to move beyond comfort and into mission. The same Spirit who hovered over the waters of creation, who overshadowed Mary at the Annunciation, and who filled the apostles at Pentecost now rests upon each of us. The oil of chrism is the outward sign, but the invisible grace is the Spirit Himself, dwelling within us and urging us to live boldly for Christ.

Eric & Bishop Charles

WHEN NETS FEEL EMPTY: LONELINESS IN OUR TIME

I recall a tragic story of a teenage girl named Sadie who took part in her church's live Nativity play. Outwardly, all seemed well. But on Christmas Day, she ended her life. Only afterward did her family discover through friends and social media the depth of her hidden struggles. This heartbreak reminds us of the danger of isolation, whether through despair, silence, or the belief that we must carry our burdens alone.

Christianity, at its heart, calls us to unity, love, and mutual support. Saint Paul reminds us to "bear one another's burdens, and so fulfill the law of Christ."[2] This is more than a suggestion; it is the lifeblood of the Church. To be part of a school of fish one must notice when another is straying or struggling and swim alongside him until he is restored.

In our parishes, workplaces, and families, this means creating space for authentic relationships in which vulnerability is met with compassion, not judgment. It means being attentive to signs of suffering, listening with patience, and offering companionship to the lonely. To be Christ's disciples is to be His hands and feet in the world, reminding others, especially the lost and forsaken, that they are never truly alone.

SWIMMING AGAINST THE CURRENT

Many of us know what it feels like to swim against the current, to face trials believing we must rely on our own strength. I have wrestled with this myself, convincing myself that I could manage life's challenges alone. Yet Paul reminds us of a greater truth: "I can do all things through Christ who strengthens me."[3]

In hindsight, we often realize that God's grace was carrying us all along, even when we felt most abandoned. These moments invite us to trust more deeply and let His strength become our strength.

And yet, despite living in an era of constant global connection, loneliness persists. A Gallup study found that one in five people worldwide, roughly 23%, report feeling lonely.[4] This startling reality

---

[2] Gal. 6:2

[3] Phil. 4:13

[4] Jeffrey M. Jones, "People Worldwide Feel Lonely — a Lot," *Gallup*, October 16, 2024, https://news.gallup.com/poll/646718/people-worldwide-feel-lonely-lot.aspx.

reflects not just social disconnection, but a spiritual hunger for true communion.

The Christian response is not withdrawal but invitation. To be a disciple is to walk alongside others, sharing Christ's love in tangible ways. The Gospel of John describes the unbreakable net of discipleship, wide enough to hold everyone (Jn. 21:11). Our task is to help others see that Jesus Himself is that net, strong enough to hold us all, even when we are weary.

BUILDING COMMUNITY IN LOVE

Authentic Christianity is about a relationship with God and with one another. We are called not only to profess faith but to extend companionship, especially to those who feel forgotten.

It was through a personal invitation to a small faith-sharing group (to which I still belong) that I first grew deeper in my faith. Such invitations remind us that the Church is not an institution of strangers but a family of disciples. Our call is to reach out, not waiting for others to come to us, but stepping into their lives with Christ's love.

This can be as simple as listening. I recall an older coworker who had lost his spouse. Though consumed by grief, he found comfort in sharing his sorrow. By offering a listening ear and a compassionate heart, I discovered that ministry often begins not with answers but simply with presence.

Jesus Himself modeled this in the simplest of ways: meals. He broke bread with tax collectors, sinners, and disciples alike. Around the table, barriers fell, relationships deepened, and grace was revealed. In the Eucharist, this truth is brought to perfection as Christ's presence is shared as both gift and banquet. Each Mass sends us forth to extend that same communion into our homes, workplaces, and neighborhoods.

To live as a school of fish is to swim together in love, each of us using our gifts to strengthen the whole. As Saint Paul reminds us, "There are different kinds of gifts, but the same Spirit distributes them."[5] Unity does not erase diversity; it sanctifies it, weaving our differences into harmony for the sake of the Gospel.

THE CALL TO VIRTUE (FAITH, HOPE, AND CHARITY)

Virtue is the steady habit of choosing the good. The Catechism teaches that faith, hope, and charity, the theological virtues, orient us directly to God (CCC 1812). Of these, charity holds the primacy: "Above all, charity binds everything together in perfect harmony."[6]

CHARITY

Charity is not sentiment but action, the decision to love as Christ loves. It calls us to feed both body and soul, as in the miracle of the loaves and fish. Before revealing Himself, Jesus often met people's immediate needs. So too, our discipleship begins with simple acts of compassion, a meal shared, a shoulder offered, a hand extended.

HUMILITY AS THE FOUNDATION

Charity requires humility, the virtue that grounds all others. At the Eucharist, we kneel together as one body, confessing our dependence on God. As Saint Paul reminds us, "Do not think of yourself more

---

[5] 1 Cor. 12:4
[6] Col. 3:14

highly than you ought."[7] Humility transforms pride into service, making us reflections of Christ who, though divine, chose the manger and the cross.

FAITH AND HOPE

Faith anchors us in trust like the woman who was healed by touching Jesus' garment, or Job, who endured intense suffering without cursing God. Jesus tells us that even faith as small as a mustard seed unleashes God's power.

Hope, meanwhile, points our eyes forward, sustaining us when we feel we are being drowned by our trials. Mary's "yes" to God and Joseph's quiet obedience reveal the courage of hope, rooted not in certainty but in trust that God will provide.

Together, these virtues form the net that holds us fast in Christ. They guide us into harmony with one another so that we may swim not as scattered fish but as a school, united in the Spirit.

The life of a disciple requires not just belief but practice. The theological virtues of faith, hope, and charity are lived out in daily choices that shape us into Christ's likeness. To remain in harmony, like a school of fish, we must continually renew our trust in God, extend compassion to others, and anchor our hope in the promise of eternal life.

The virtues of faith, hope, and charity are threads that keep the net whole. Charity feeds both the body and the soul, hope steadies us when currents grow strong, and faith anchors us to Christ. Together, they weave a net wide enough to gather all nations, a living echo of the miraculous 153 fish.

---

[7] Rom. 12:3

REFLECTION QUESTIONS FROM CHAPTER SEVEN

When have you realized that God was guiding you while you were "swimming against the current"?

Who in your life might need a personal invitation into community or companionship?

What small acts of charity can you practice daily to help build Christian unity?

How do humility, faith, and hope sustain you in your relationship with God?

ACTION STEP: SWIMMING TOGETHER IN CHRIST

Return and Renew – Recall your Baptism, Confirmation, and Eucharist as the anchors of your discipleship. Begin each day with the Sign of the Cross and entrust your life to God's grace.

Reach Out – Extend a personal invitation to someone who may feel isolated. Invite them to Mass, coffee, or a meal. Like the early Christians' fish symbol, let your life be a quiet sign of belonging and welcome.

Pray Simply – End your day with this prayer of unity:

"Lord Jesus, help me to swim not alone, but as part of Your Body, the Church. Strengthen my faith, anchor my hope, and increase my charity, so that others may find Your love through me."

Chapter Eight

Called and Caught by Christ

The Miraculous Draught of Fishes, Raphael, 1515.
Public domain.

In the Sea of Galilee, the disciples fished all night and caught nothing. Then a voice from shore called out: "Cast the net on the right side of the boat." In that simple command, the risen Jesus revealed Himself to His friends.

After the Resurrection, the disciples had slipped back into their old routines as fishermen, uncertain of what came next. Their experience mirrors our own. How often do we move through life on autopilot, working, striving, and laboring, yet feeling empty? Like the disciples, we often compartmentalize our existence: work in one box, relationships in another, faith in yet another. But Jesus steps into these ordinary spaces and breaks down the barriers we construct.

His call to trust the voice from the shore reminds us that every part of our life is meant to be gathered into His presence and transformed by His love. Peter's encounter with Jesus, in which he professes his love three times, teaches us a vital truth: we are not meant to lead but to follow. When Jesus is at the center of our lives, the blindfold of routine lifts, and we begin to glimpse the beauty for which God created us.

The disciples' experience shows that Jesus transforms ordinary moments into extraordinary encounters. The following stories, told in their own words, bear witness to this truth that God steps into human weakness, repairs broken nets, and draws us back into His love.

A JOURNEY OF GRACE AND REDEMPTION – CRYSTAL'S STORY

I'm Crystal. I was born in Chicago and moved to Texas when I was two years old. I'm the oldest of three children. My brother Mike is five and a half years younger and my youngest brother, Chase, is twenty-five years younger. My mom was only nineteen and unmarried when she became pregnant with me. Over the years, I've realized that abortion likely crossed her mind, but thank God she chose life. I was born at St. Francis Hospital and baptized at St. Hilary's Church four months later.

My parents married and settled our family in Arlington, Texas. I was shy and quiet, and I hated being away from home, which made making friends difficult. My brother Mike was my world. Growing up, we were inseparable.

The practice of faith in our family was minimal. Every weekend, we would go to Mass as a family, but that was it. I still remember my First Communion vividly; I was the only girl not wearing a veil, and I felt embarrassed.

When I was eight, my mom took me and Mike to lunch and told us she and my dad were getting a divorce. I didn't understand what divorce meant, but she made it sound exciting, like we would have freedom, fun, and McDonald's every day. When she moved out, I assumed I was going with her. But she only took Mike, my favorite person in the world. That night, it was just my dad and me when I saw him cry for the first time. That's when I began to resent my mom.

After a few months, my dad decided Mike and I shouldn't be separated, so I moved in with my mom. But she soon gave full custody of us back to my dad. For the next ten years, it was just the three of us, Dad, Mike, and me. I became a mother figure to Mike. My dad, selfless as ever, put off dating until I graduated high school in order to keep our home stable. Looking back, I realize that's where I first learned the meaning of "dying to self."

Every week, we attended Saturday evening Mass at St. Joseph in Arlington. Our house was filled with reminders of faith: pictures of

Jesus, crucifixes, the Last Supper, and a large family Bible. Yet I began to feel embarrassed about being Catholic. None of my friends went to church, and I resented missing out on Saturday nights. When I was fifteen, I started Confirmation prep but dropped out. I wasn't confirmed, and I felt ashamed of that.

Dating only deepened the shame. My first boyfriend was Jewish, and his father had forbidden him to date a Catholic. My second boyfriend belonged to the Church of Christ, and his parents also disapproved of Catholics. Though I didn't understand why, I grew embarrassed of my faith.

After high school, I stayed home to attend Texas Christian University. I thought my dad and Mike needed me. I took a Bible class, assuming it would be easy. It turned out to be one of the hardest classes I'd ever taken, and I realized how little I actually knew. That realization left me questioning the point of being Catholic.

During my senior year, I secretly married my first husband. He wasn't Catholic and disliked going to Mass, so I stopped attending. When he became verbally abusive and self- destructive, I hid it from everyone. With support from family and friends, I eventually left him, a decision I later recognized as God's protection.

A few years later, I met John on a blind date. When I found out he was Catholic, I felt relieved; I could go back to church without judgment. Our daughter, Charlotte, was born early in our relationship. I was afraid to disappoint my dad, but a supportive boss encouraged me to talk to a priest. Shortly after Charlotte's birth, John and I got married and had her baptized. But those early years were hard, financially, emotionally, and spiritually.

I began to resent John, feeling like I carried all the burdens of our marriage. When infertility set in, I grew angry at God. In that anger, I made choices that broke my marriage. When John found out, he took Charlotte and left. That moment shattered me, but also brought me to my knees. Through counseling, prayer, and time, we slowly healed.

We eventually moved to Southlake, and found a new church home at Good Shepherd. My faith reignited. Bible Study fellowship deepened my understanding of Scripture. Leading faith formation with John strengthened my relationship with God. During a youth retreat, I experienced the Holy Spirit in a way that changed everything, and finally faced the Confirmation I had long avoided. Last year, I was confirmed, with my daughter Charlotte as my sponsor.

Today, my faith is stronger than ever. Daily Mass, prayer, and community have transformed my life. My brother Mike now attends Mass regularly and is preparing for Confirmation; his daughters will be baptized this summer. John and I are celebrating twenty years of marriage, and I am no longer ashamed of my Catholic faith.

Through my journey, I've learned that God's grace never stops chasing us. My hope is that Charlotte will never feel ashamed of her faith but will trust in God's love, no matter where life leads.

HOME AT LAST – MIKE'S STORY

My name is Mike. I was a born-again Christian for over thirty years. When COVID lockdowns began, I couldn't attend church, but truthfully, I had already started drifting away. I still believed but had grown disillusioned with "church."

My daughter runs the children's liturgy at her Catholic parish. She asked me to help with a pilgrimage to the Catholic National Shrine & Basilica of Our Lady in Walsingham. I agreed, not thinking much of it. But around that same time, my father-in-law was hospitalized. My wife asked me to bring my laptop to the hospital so she could watch Easter Mass with him. I set up the stream, and saw him cry the entire time he watched, making the sign of the cross again and again. It was profoundly moving. When I returned home, I broke down sobbing. Something within me had shifted.

A few weeks later, my daughters held a cake sale for their World Youth Day trip. I hadn't planned to attend Mass that day, but as I walked around town, I felt a quiet urge to go. Something in the homily resonated deeply. That night, I dreamed I was praying the Hail Mary, over and over.

The next day, I secretly ordered An Idiot's Guide to Catholicism on my Kindle and couldn't put it down. My wife noticed my late-night reading and asked what I was studying. When I told her, she was stunned, but supportive. Soon, I was full of questions about the faith.

We later visited Walsingham again, providentially arriving during the New Dawn conference. Watching Catholics worship so passionately broke every stereotype I'd held. I wept openly. Soon, I began attending Mass with my wife. I went up for blessings during Communion, thanking Jesus each time for His sacrifice.

One day, during Eucharistic Adoration, I was moved to tears again. My wife went to confession, and I felt a deep, almost painful longing to do the same, but couldn't yet. After meeting with our priest, I began RCIA. At the Easter Vigil this year, I was received fully into the Catholic Church.

Looking back, I see the Holy Spirit's hand guiding me home all along. Every tear, every nudge, every "yes" brought me closer to Jesus. I can only say: Thank You, Lord.

THE MISSING PIECE – ERIC'S STORY

I grew up in a Catholic home, a cradle Catholic who believed in the Church's core teachings, but always felt like something was missing. I knew the Eucharist was Christ's true presence, yet my prayer life fluctuated. Even so, I was drawn to contemplative prayer and the Rosary.

As a teen, I volunteered in parish ministry, which eventually led me to the diocesan seminary. After several years, I discerned that God was not calling me to the priesthood. But still, that sense of "something missing" remained.

I sought answers through career and self-reliance, but fear kept me from surrendering. In prayer and Adoration, I often wrestled with God, asking "Why me, Lord? Am I worthy?"

My grandfather once told me, "Find a good Catholic wife and settle down." In marriage to Angela and fatherhood of our daughter Abigail, I discovered that blessing. Slowly, my fear of dependence turned into trust. My heart of stone began to soften into a heart of flesh (Ez. 36:26).

The early years of marriage were challenging, with a new baby, bills, and stress. When I fell ill and was hospitalized, I discovered the writings of St. Josemaría Escrivá. One line pierced me: "God is not removing you from your environment... But he wants you to be a saint right there."[1]

That insight reframed everything. Holiness wasn't somewhere else; it was here. Later, during a painful battle with sciatica, I turned to Isaiah 53 and the Passion narratives. My suffering was a sharing in Christ's cross. My self-reliance began to break, and I found peace in surrender.

---

[1] "Saint Josemaría Escrivá," *Opus Dei*, https://opusdei.org/en-us/saint-josemaria/.

Accepting my cross, I discovered joy in small sacrifices. The burden grew lighter. I realized that what I'd been missing was not purpose, but love.

Today, I see that, even in my imperfections, God has been forming me. Like the apostles, I've learned that discipleship isn't about perfection, but persistence. Christ transforms weakness into witness.

THE UPPER ROOM – THE SOLEMNITY OF PENTECOST

Come, Holy Spirit, fill the hearts of Your faithful and enkindle in them the fire of Your love. Send forth Your Spirit, and they shall be created, and You shall renew the face of the earth.[2]

Discipleship means our efforts succeed with Christ but fail without Him. Jesus sees where the fish are, directs us where to cast, and strengthens the net so that none are lost. Crystal's, Mike's, and my own journeys are all stories of being drawn into that same net, sometimes broken, sometimes hesitant, but always caught by His mercy.

Jesus' question to Peter, "Do you love me?" still echoes through time. Every yes restores and sends us out again to cast into the deep. Every cast matters, every small act of kindness, every whispered prayer, and every act of forgiveness. Some days the catch feels small; other days, the net bursts with abundance.

What matters is our willingness to keep casting, trusting the gaze of the Fisherman.

God's love is constant, always ready to welcome us back. Faith is not merely a set of doctrines but a living relationship with the God

---

[2] Ps. 104:30

who loves us deeply. When we open our hearts to His call and trust in His grace, we begin to taste the fullness of life He promises.

The Upper Room -
The Solemnity of Pentecost.
Courtesy of Christine Barrantes.

REFLECTION QUESTIONS FROM CHAPTER EIGHT

How has God transformed your life? In what ways has His presence shaped your journey and deepened your understanding of His love and grace?

What is your testimony of faith as a Christian disciple? How did your life look before you came to know Jesus, and how has it changed since you invited Him to be the center of your life?

If you do not yet have a testimony of faith, consider this: If one day, you should meet Saint Peter and the communion of saints, would they recognize you as a disciple by the life you lived? If not, how might you begin living out your faith and writing your testimony today? Perhaps Jesus is already asking you to trust Him, inviting you to a small act, a prayer, or a simple choice. The question is: will you have the courage to heed His call?

ACTION STEP: ENCOUNTERING JESUS IN DAILY LIFE

Return – Choose one ordinary area of your life, such as work, chores, school, or family time, and consciously invite Jesus into it this week. Say: "Lord, walk with me here."

Renew – Reflect on your personal testimony. Write down one moment when you experienced God's grace, whether in struggle, healing, or joy. Keep it short and simple, a reminder of how He has worked in your life.

Reach Out – Share your story with someone: a family member, a friend, or a parish small group. Testimonies, like Peter's encounter with the risen Christ, encourage others to believe that God is alive and active today.

Pray Simply – End each day this week with prayer: "Come, Holy Spirit. Enkindle in me the fire of Your love. Renew my heart and guide my steps closer to Jesus."

Chapter Nine

The Spirit's Gifts
for Mission

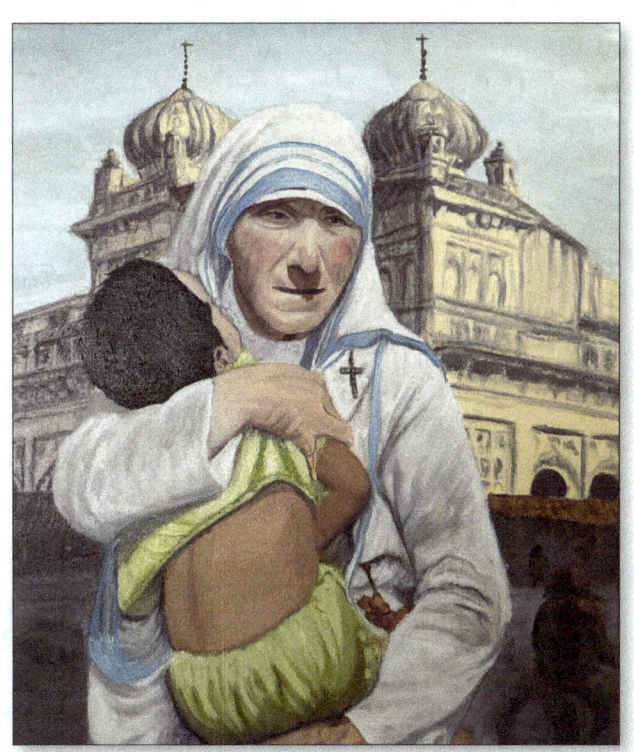

Saint Mother Teresa of Calcutta.
Courtesy of Christine Barrantes.

We can only imagine the beauty of the moment when Jesus' disciples caught a multitude of fish. If you've ever visited an aquarium or watched a koi pond, you know how mesmerizing it is when fish move in harmony through water. In much the same way, we, God's "catch of fish," are drawn into this world for a reason and a purpose, each uniquely created to contribute to His divine plan.

Our lives are like a finely woven tapestry, a masterpiece crafted by God to reveal His glory to a world longing for beauty and meaning. As Saint Paul reminds us, "We are His handiwork, created in Christ Jesus for the good works that God has prepared in advance, that we should live in them."[1]

In my parish, a monthly stewardship reminder titled "Sharing Our Joy" encourages us as disciples to offer our time, talents, and treasure for the good of others. This call challenges us to reflect on how we can use what we've been given for God's glory.

Giftedness is one of the most remarkable facets of human existence, a testament to the Creator's generosity. Every person possesses unique abilities and resources, even if they sometimes go unnoticed. Yet these gifts are not meant to remain dormant or self-serving. They are entrusted to us as stewards, called to nurture, share, and multiply them in service of a higher purpose.

In the Parable of the Talents (Mt 25:14-30), Jesus underscores this responsibility. The master praises the servants who multiplied their talents but rebukes the one who buried his out of fear. The lesson is clear: giftedness is not merely a privilege but a responsibility, a call to action. To bury a gift is to deny the intention of the Giver, who calls us to glorify Him through our service to others.

---

[1] Eph. 2:10

Giftedness and stewardship are inseparable. To embrace one is to acknowledge the other. Stewardship sanctifies our gifts, channeling them into acts of love, justice, and compassion. Through them, we fulfill the divine invitation to be co-creators with God, multiplying goodness in the world and preparing for the ultimate commendation: "Well done, good and faithful servant."[2]

OUR CALL TO STEWARDSHIP

Stewardship is a profound expression of faith, a response of gratitude, responsibility, and love to the gifts God has entrusted to us. If you already volunteer your time and talents in ministry, you are living this call. Whether through teaching, music, organization, or quiet service, your offering strengthens the body of Christ and deepens your own spiritual growth.

If you haven't yet found your place in ministry, this is your invitation to ask: Where is God calling me to serve? What gifts has He placed within me that are waiting to be shared? The answer is often found in what brings you joy or moves your heart. God doesn't call everyone to the same task; He calls each of us to the work we were created for.

Think back to a moment when you found joy in giving, perhaps a small act of kindness, a handmade gift, or a project that touched someone's life. The joy that followed wasn't merely emotional; it was spiritual. It was the Holy Spirit working through love, revealing a glimpse of divine joy. God is the ultimate giver, and when we give, we reflect His very nature.

Stepping into stewardship transforms the way we see time, talent, and treasure, recognizing them not as possessions to guard but as gifts

---

[2] Mt. 25:21

to share. It reshapes our priorities and draws us closer to the life Jesus promised. Most of all, it aligns our hearts with God's, opening us to the grace and joy that come from living out His mission.

This joy is renewed at every Mass, where we receive the supreme gift of grace in the Eucharist. The Incarnation reminds us that we were made for more than this world

alone. Through the Holy Spirit, we are strengthened to live lives of grace and generosity.

Let us, then, embrace the call to stewardship to become vessels of joy, grace, and love, sharing the gifts God has so freely given us with a world yearning for His beauty and truth.

ACKNOWLEDGING OUR GIFTS

The word charism comes from the Greek charisma, meaning "a favor" or "a gift." These spiritual gifts are bestowed upon us at Baptism (cf. CCC #799). They are not meant for personal gain but for building up the Church and glorifying God (cf. CCC #799, #951).

Each baptized Christian receives unique charisms and spiritual gifts, yet these gifts require faithful attention like a field that must be tended. Through prayer, discernment, and action, we learn how to use them for the service of the Church and the good of the world. When we embrace our role as disciples, we participate in advancing the Kingdom of Heaven on earth and live as citizens of God's eternal kingdom.

The Holy Spirit plays these gifts within us like finely tuned instruments, composing a symphony of grace for the good of humanity. Have you ever witnessed someone using their charisma? Perhaps you've seen the gift of healing bring restoration to a loved one or been moved by an evangelist whose words turned hearts to Christ. Such moments reveal the Spirit at work, tangible evidence that God continues to build His Church through His people.

At Baptism, we are drawn into a communion of charisms, becoming new creations in Christ. These gifts enable us to live out the threefold mission of priest, prophet, and king:

Priest: We are called to live sacrificially, uniting our daily actions to Christ's will. Through the sacraments and faithful living in our homes, workplaces, and communities, we become *alter Christus*, another Christ in the world.

Prophet: We are commissioned to proclaim the truth of the Gospel with courage and conviction, calling others to conversion and life in Christ.

King: Reflecting the crown of thorns worn by Jesus, we lead through humility and service. In our families, churches, and communities, we mirror the love and justice of our eternal King.

Each of these roles, animated by the Spirit's charisms, allows us to bring Christ to others in distinctive and powerful ways. Let us discern how to embrace these gifts fully, live faithfully as disciples, and build up the Church for the glory of God.

DISCERNING AND EMBRACING OUR CHARISMS

To recognize our charisms, we must remain open to the Holy Spirit's quiet work within us. I remember, as a child, watching televangelists claim miraculous healings. Such displays often breed skepticism, but true charisms are never about spectacle; they are exercised humbly, for the good of others, and always in charity (cf. CCC #800).

The Catechism teaches that the Holy Spirit "distributes special graces among the faithful of every rank"[3] for the building up of the Church. They are a Communion of Charisms, for these gifts bestowed from the Holy Spirit are not for self-promotion but for the service of others and the unity of the Body of Christ.

I once attended a Called & Gifted workshop by the Catherine of Siena Institute, co-founded by Sherry Weddell (author of Forming Intentional Disciples) and the Western Dominican Province. The experience was eye-opening. After completing a spiritual gifts inventory, I discovered certain areas of strength, but I also learned that discernment requires more than just results. It demands prayer and guidance from a spiritual mentor.

For instance, I might excel in administration professionally, but that doesn't mean I possess the charism of administration. Likewise, a natural talent for sharing the faith does not automatically equate to the charism of evangelization. Charisms are not simply natural abilities; they are supernatural graces given for the building up of the Church.

Discerning them takes prayer, reflection, and guidance, often from a priest, deacon, or trained spiritual director. As we grow in awareness of our gifts, we come to see that each is an invitation to serve, to love, and to participate more fully in God's mission in the world.

HOLINESS IN DAILY WORK

In the quiet rhythm of our daily work, we are given countless moments to glorify God. When we learn to pause within our tasks and gently attend to His presence, even the most ordinary actions

---

[3] CCC 951

are transformed. What we do with our hands becomes sacred, not because the work is extraordinary, but because God is near.

Labor is no longer merely a means of survival or productivity. It becomes an offering laid quietly before God, an act of love shaped by time and effort, a prayer woven into the hours of the day. In this way, work does not only shape the world around us, it slowly forms the heart within us.

I see this in my wife, Angela, who works in the bakery department of a grocery store. During the Christmas season, she carries her work home with her, not as burden but as joy, preparing a treasured family recipe of fig cookies. What begins in the rhythm of daily labor becomes a gift, filling our home with warmth, memory, and delight. So too, our own work, when received and offered with love, is meant not only to sustain our lives, but to awaken joy and to bless others through the quiet faithfulness of our hands.

Both the current pontiff, Pope Leo XIV, and his namesake, Pope Leo XIII, especially in *Rerum Novarum*, remind us that human work belongs to the dignity of creation itself. Through the fruit of our hands and the sweat of our brow, we participate in the creative mystery of the image and likeness of God. As God once spoke creation into being, so now He invites us to share in His ongoing work, sanctifying the world through faithful and attentive labor.

The Benedictine tradition of Ora et Labora (Prayer and Work) captures this integration beautifully. It teaches that prayer and work are not opposing forces but complementary expressions of one spiritual life. Through prayer, we draw near to God, seeking His guidance and grace. Through work, we embody that grace, serving others and reflecting God's creative love. Together, they form a path to holiness, in which every effort, no matter how ordinary, becomes an offering to God.

Sr. Joan Chittister, OSB, reminds us that work is not merely utilitarian but is a participation in God's ongoing act of creation. She writes, "Creative and productive work are simply meant to enhance the Garden and sustain us while we grow in God."[4] Work, viewed through this lens, is not a burden but a blessing we share in the divine project of creation. When we align our efforts with God's purpose, our labor becomes part of His redemptive plan.

In today's culture, where identity is often tied to career, Chittister's insight feels especially urgent, "Once the retirement dinner is over and the company watch is engraved, there has to be something left in life that makes us human and makes us happy, or life may well have been in vain."[5]

If our work leaves us empty or restless, perhaps the issue is not the work itself but our awareness of God's presence within that work. A contemplative posture, in which we pause throughout the day to offer our tasks to God, transforms even the mundane into a sacred encounter.

Jean-François Millet's painting *The Angelus*, depicting two farmers pausing in prayer over their labor, captures this perfectly. Their prayer sanctifies their work. In their stillness, they mirror the Creator, blending productivity with reverence.

Practically, this means approaching every task with gratitude, integrity, and intention. Whether tending a family, pursuing a career, or serving others, each moment can become a doorway to holiness. When infused with prayer and attentiveness to God's presence, even

---

[4] Joan Chittister, The Rule of Benedict: A Spirituality for the 21st Century (New York: Crossroad Publishing, 1992), 214.
[5] Ibid

routine labor becomes a profound act of grace, one that draws both worker and world closer to the heart of Christ.

LIVING OUR HEAVENLY CALLING ON EARTH

President John F. Kennedy once said, "Ask not what your country can do for you, ask what you can do for your country."[6] The same principle applies to our spiritual lives. As baptized and confirmed Christians, our true citizenship is not of this world but of heaven. We are called to live so that our lives reflect the joy, love, and grace of God's kingdom here and now.

Saint Paul wrote, "Our citizenship is in heaven, and from it we await a Savior, the Lord Jesus Christ."[7] This heavenly identity challenges us to live as stewards of God's kingdom, not passive observers. The Church on earth is a reflection of heaven, and we are called to nurture it through our time, gifts, and presence.

At times, we may feel disheartened by imperfections within the Church, by others' failings, or our own frustrations. Yet even these moments are invitations to deeper participation. Rather than standing apart in criticism, we might ask, "Is the Holy Spirit prompting me to serve more actively?" Perhaps that quiet dissatisfaction is God's gentle call to step forward in ministry or leadership.

True stewardship requires moving beyond comfort or convenience. It is not merely giving from abundance but offering our hearts, our time, and our hands for the sake of others. Living as citizens of

[6] John F. Kennedy, *Inaugural Address*, January 20, 1961, John F. Kennedy Presidential Library and Museum, https://www.jfklibrary.org/learn/about-jfk/historic-speeches/inaugural-address.

[7] Phil. 3:20

heaven means bringing its values, mercy, justice, and humility into our daily choices.

Every act of stewardship bridges heaven and earth. By offering our talents in prayer, service, and love, we make visible the invisible kingdom of God. We care not only for

the material needs of the Church but also for her spiritual unity and vitality.

To "cast the net," as Jesus commands, is to rediscover our discipleship and use our charisms in service of God's will. Without Christ as our compass, we lose direction; with Him, even ordinary moments become mission fields of grace.

Saint James reminds us, "Every good and perfect gift comes from above, from the Father of lights. He willed to give us birth by the word of truth that we may be a kind of first fruits of His creatures."[8]

Let us, then, embrace our heavenly calling here on earth. When our work and witness align with God's will, they become sacred acts of love, illuminating the world with His presence and drawing all creation closer to its divine fulfillment.

REFLECTION QUESTIONS FROM CHAPTER NINE

Reflect and meditate on how God has crafted you as a fine and exquisite masterpiece, a unique thread in His divine tapestry, designed to live as a Christian disciple.

What does Christian stewardship mean to you? How do you give back to the Church, not only within its walls but also in your home and wider community?

---

[8] Jas. 1:17-18

Reflect on the Communion of Charisms. How has your baptismal call equipped and inspired you to be a witness of Christ in the world?

Consider taking a spiritual gifts inventory offered through the Called & Gifted platform by the Catherine of Siena Institute or online. Many online resources exist. Begin with the Appendix Section Survey – Journey With Christ in order to see where you are at in your spiritual journey before proceeding with such a task.

Reflect on the nature of work. How can you make your labor more meaningful by contemplating its creative and redemptive role in God's plan?

Meditate on how God has chosen you from the moment of your conception to this very day (cf. Jas 1:17–18). How can you continue to let Jesus be your compass, guiding and leading you to accomplish His will as His chosen disciple?

ACTION STEP: SHARING OUR GIFTS FOR GOD'S GLORY

Return – Recall your baptismal call. Begin each morning this week by slowly making the Sign of the Cross, thanking God for the unique gifts and charisms He has placed within you.

Renew – Take one intentional step toward discerning your gifts. Pray with Ephesians 2:10 ("We are His handiwork..."), or complete a spiritual gifts inventory, asking the Holy Spirit to reveal how He desires you to serve.

Reach Out – Use one of your natural or spiritual gifts in service of another person this week, whether in your parish, your family, or your workplace. Even the smallest act of generosity can be a true expression of stewardship.

Pray Simply – End your day with this prayer of surrender:

"Lord Jesus, You are the giver of every good gift. Help me to use my time, talents, and treasure for Your glory and the good of Your Church. Make me a faithful steward of the blessings You have entrusted to me."

Chapter Ten

Drawn by the Word of God

Family Bible. Photo by author.

Afisherman's lure is carefully crafted not to harm, but to draw in through its bright colors. In the spiritual life, Scripture is God's great lure for the soul. It catches our attention through truth and beauty, captivating the heart and leading it toward a deeper relationship with Him. Unlike worldly lures that deceive, the lure of God's Word draws us toward eternal life and anchors us in His love.

The Psalmist declares, "Your word is a lamp to my feet and a light to my path."[1] Just as a fisherman casts his lure and waits patiently, God casts His Word into the waters of our hearts, inviting us to take hold and be caught up in His mercy. Every page of Scripture is a living invitation, not static ink on paper, but the living breath of God (cf. 2 Tim. 3:16-17).

Even Jesus, the Eternal Word made flesh, turned to Scripture when He faced temptation in the desert. Three times, He answered Satan with the words of Deuteronomy (Mt. 4:1- 11). If the Son of God relied on the Word to withstand trial, how much more do we need to let Scripture become the lure that strengthens and sustains us?

ENGAGING WITH SCRIPTURE DAILY

For many, reading the Bible can feel daunting. Where do we start? How do we move from seeing the Bible as a heavy book on a shelf to hearing it as the living voice of God?

One practice that has transformed our home is praying the Divine Office, the Liturgy of the Hours. This ancient rhythm of psalms, Scripture, and prayer sanctifies the day through moments of praise: the Office of Readings, Morning Prayer (Lauds), Daytime Prayer (Terce, Sext, None), Evening Prayer (Vespers), and Night Prayer

---

[1] Ps. 119:105

(Compline). Our busy lives don't allow us to pray every office, but Morning Prayer and Compline have become anchors that center our family in God's Word.

Another treasured practice is Lectio Divina, which my wife and I discovered through a Catholic young adult group while dating. Tom, the group's leader, introduced us to this ancient and beautiful method of praying with Scripture. Its four steps are simple, yet life-changing:

- *Read (Lectio)* – Slowly read the passage, allowing its words to echo in your heart.
- *Meditate (Meditatio)* – Reflect on a phrase or word that stands out.
- *Pray (Oratio)* – Speak to God from your heart about what you've heard.
- *Contemplate (Contemplatio)* – Rest in silence, letting His Word dwell within you.

Lectio Divina turns Scripture from text into conversation. It reminds us that the Word is not merely something to study, it is Someone to encounter. Tools like daily Mass readings, Scripture apps, or small Bible study groups can help establish this rhythm. Even ten minutes each morning spent with a Gospel passage can open the heart to grace.

PERSONAL TESTIMONIES OF GOD'S WORD

There have been moments in my own life when Scripture became the precise lure I needed. In a season of fear and confusion, I opened to Isaiah and read: "Do not fear, for I have redeemed you; I have called you by name, you are mine."[2] Those words pierced my heart. I knew in that instant that God was speaking directly to me.

---

[2] Is. 43:1

Saint Augustine experienced the same divine pull. Restless and uncertain, he opened the Scriptures and read Romans 13:13-14: "Put on the Lord Jesus Christ, and make no provision for the desires of the flesh." That one verse became the lure that drew him from sin to sanctity.

Our family has also been caught by the Word's gentle net. At my niece's baptism, the Gospel reading "Let the children come to me"[3] struck me deeply. It reminded me that every child baptized into the Church is held securely in Christ's unbreakable net, no matter where life may lead.

SCRIPTURE IN LITURGY AND HOME

Every Mass overflows with the lure of Scripture; every reading is placed with purpose. The Old Testament prepares the heart, the Psalms give voice to prayer, the New Testament exhorts, and the Gospel brings us face to face with Christ.

Yet Scripture is not meant for Sunday alone. It is intended to dwell in our homes and shape our families. Some simple ways to weave it into daily life:

- Read a Psalm together before dinner.
- Memorize one short verse as a family each week.
- Keep an open Bible in a visible place as a sign that God's voice lives among you.

Even small habits bear fruit. The Word of God is not reserved for theologians or clergy; it is the lure of love cast into every soul, calling each of us, young and old alike, into the depths of divine friendship.

---

[3] Mk. 10:13-16

OVERCOMING RESISTANCE

Many people avoid Scripture because they fear they won't understand it. Yet the Word of God was never meant to be locked away. The same Spirit who inspired the sacred authors to write Scripture also encourages us to understand it today. When a passage feels confusing, bring it to prayer and echo the words of Samuel: "Speak, Lord, your servant is listening."[4]

Scripture also meets us in seasons of dryness. At times, the net feels empty, and our reading seems fruitless. But just as the disciples were told to cast their nets again, we too must persist. Every reading plants a seed, even if its growth remains unseen.

The lure of Scripture is gentle yet powerful. It draws us from darkness into light, from confusion into clarity, from despair into hope. When we allow God's Word to "catch" us, we discover that it is not we who are holding onto the Bible; it is the living Word of God holding onto us.

Like the disciples on the Sea of Galilee, our nets may at first feel empty. But when we trust the voice of Christ and cast again into the waters of His Word, we will find abundance beyond measure, grace, wisdom, and the very presence of God Himself.

REFLECTION QUESTIONS FROM CHAPTER TEN

What passage of Scripture has most influenced your daily life, and why?

---

[4] 1 Sam. 3:9

Do you find it difficult to pray with the Bible? What helps you overcome this?

How can you bring Scripture more intentionally into your family or friendships?

When you feel spiritually dry, are you willing to cast your net again by opening God's Word?

In what ways has Scripture acted as a lure in your life, drawing you back to Christ when you drift?

ACTION STEP: LETTING GOD'S WORD TRANSFORM YOUR HEART

Return – Begin or end each day with Scripture. Keep a Bible in a visible place in your home. Before you scroll, check the headlines, or fall asleep, read at least one verse, perhaps the daily Gospel or a Psalm. Let God's Word become your first or final thought.

Renew – Try a new way of praying with Scripture this week:
- Practice Lectio Divina with a Gospel passage.
- Join others in Morning or Evening Prayer from the
- Liturgy of the Hours.
- Write a verse that inspires you on a note and place it
- where you'll see it often.

Reach Out – Share God's Word with someone else. Text a verse that encouraged you, pray a Psalm with your family before a meal, or invite a friend to a Bible study. Even a small invitation can draw another soul closer to Christ.

Pray Simply – "Speak, Lord, your servant is listening. Let Your Word be the lamp that guides my path, and the lure that draws me deeper into Your love."

Chapter Eleven

Raising Christian Guppies and Lambs

*Stained glass at St. John the Baptist's Anglican Church,
Ashfield, New South Wales. Public domain.*

Our journey of faith begins in childhood. Jesus makes this clear when He says, "Let the children come to me... for the kingdom of heaven belongs to such as these."[1] Children trust easily, forgive quickly, and depend entirely on others. That same childlike trust is what God calls us to rediscover as adults in relation to Him. He calls us to lean on Him, to rest in His care, and to allow His grace to carry us.

In John's Gospel, the Risen Jesus calls to His disciples on the shore: "Children, do you have anything to eat?"[2] That tender question reminds us that we depend on God not only for daily bread but for every spiritual grace.

TRADITIONS THAT NURTURE FAITH

In our family, we try to make faith something tangible, visible, lived, and celebrated. We mark baptismal anniversaries, honor the feast days of saints, and bring prayer into everyday spaces.

Celebrating a special Marian Solemnity.
Photo by Angela Stengel.

---

[1] Mt. 19:14
[2] Jn. 21:5

One Lent, my wife and daughter used sidewalk chalk to draw the Stations of the Cross on the pavement in front of our home. Neighbors slowed down as they passed; a few even stopped to look. That simple act transformed ordinary concrete into holy ground, a reminder that faith doesn't stay inside church walls. It spills into streets, homes, and hearts wherever love is expressed.

Preparation for the Sacrament of Reconciliation, or Penance, has also become a cherished family routine. Before we go, we sit together with our daughter and use a children's examination of conscience as a simple yet profound way to prepare all our hearts. In that moment, we remind one another that mercy is not abstract; it is the living embrace of God's love.

Pietro Antonio Novelli, 1779. Public domain.

As Pietro Antonio Novelli's artwork beautifully portrays, in Confession, one soul, who has not yet confessed, remains bound by chains while another, absolved, is led away by an angel. That is what the Sacrament offers: freedom, peace, and a new beginning. By seeking forgiveness ourselves and teaching our children to do the same, we pass on a living faith rooted in mercy.

TENDING OUR LITTLE FLOCK

As noted above, the Church calls the family the "domestic church." Parents, grandparents, and godparents are the first catechists, entrusted with feeding the "little lambs." After asking Peter, "Do you love me?" Jesus instructs him, "Feed my lambs."[3] If we do not feed our children spiritually, the world will feed them something else. That is why we keep Bibles in our homes, pray together, and strive, however imperfectly, to live what we profess.

Children's questions often open doors to deeper faith. When my daughter once asked, "Who made God?" I smiled, recognizing how her simple wonder echoed centuries of theology. The curiosity of children is not something to suppress but to nurture with honesty, patience, and joy. Alongside dreams of careers and vocations, we must plant another dream: sainthood.

Eric as Saint Mark the Evangelist &
Daughter Abigail as Saint Thérèse of Lisieux.

---

[3] Jn. 21:15

NO EXCUSES FOR MASS

The Eucharist is the "source and summit" of our faith (CCC 1324). Yet how often do excuses creep in?

Too busy? Then give God the very time you think you don't have.

Hurt by the Church? Healing begins with Christ Himself.

Children restless at Mass? Let them come; grace is absorbed even in fidgeting.

Doubt or disbelief? The Mass is where questions meet answers.

Don't feel like it? Love is not a feeling; it's faithfulness.

Broken and shared, Jesus, the Bread of Life, makes us whole.
Courtesy of Christine Barrantes

AWE FOR THE EUCHARIST

Mass is heaven on earth. Preparing beforehand by reading the Scriptures for the day or pausing to say a prayer before entering the church helps us enter more deeply into that mystery.

Eucharistic Adoration is another powerful practice, even for children. In silence, they learn that God does not always shout; sometimes,

He simply waits with love. There, in stillness, Jesus whispers: "Come to me, all you who labor and are burdened, and I will give you rest."[4]

As a family, we sometimes pray the Anima Christi after Communion. Its words remind us that the Eucharist is not symbolic but a living encounter with Christ Himself:

Soul of Christ, sanctify me…

Body of Christ, save me…

Within Your wounds, hide me…

At the hour of my death, call me, And bid me come to You,

That with Your saints I may praise You forever and ever.

Amen.

OUR CALL TO SAINTHOOD

If we do not show our children that sainthood is possible, who will? Holiness is not perfection; it is saying "yes" to Jesus again and again in the ordinary moments of life.

Even the hidden saints, those whose names we do not know, remind us that holiness often grows quietly, like seeds in the soil. Their example tells our children (and us): You, too, can be a saint.

PRAYER TO SAINTS WHOM NOBODY KNOWS ABOUT

Thank you, Unknown Saints, for living a life in service of God.

Thank you for your quiet, humble witness. You are living with Him now.

I may not know your name, but I ask you to please pray for [insert intentions].

---

[4] Mt. 11:28

Please take my intentions to the feet of God. And ask that they be given favorable outcomes. If His answer differs from my desire, grant me the grace to obey His perfect will.

I hope to meet you one day in Heaven.

In Jesus' name, I pray. Amen.

REFLECTION QUESTIONS FROM CHAPTER ELEVEN

How does faith live in my home? What do my children or loved ones see in me that points them to Christ?

Do I carve out daily time for prayer alone or with family, or do I let busyness crowd it out?

What small traditions (like prayer before meals or celebrating baptism anniversaries or saint feast days) could I begin or renew in my home?

When I attend Mass, do I prepare my heart or simply show up?

How might I recover a sense of awe for the Eucharist?

Have I ever tried attending Eucharistic Adoration? If not, what holds me back, and what might I experience if I simply sit in His presence?

ACTION STEP: NURTURING FAITH AT HOME

This week, choose one way to plant or water seeds of faith in your home:

Return – Remember your First Holy Communion. Approach Jesus in the Eucharist this week with the same awe you felt that day.

Renew – Recommit to one family tradition: a Rosary, celebrating a feast day, or going to Confession together. Let it become an anchor of faith.

Reach Out – Place a simple sign of faith, a crucifix, an open Bible, or a holy image in a central spot in your home. Let it speak silently to visitors and remind your family of your roots.

Pray Simply – "Jesus, You said, 'Let the children come to me.' Teach me to guide my family with love and patience. Help me raise saints, little by little, through everyday love."

Chapter Twelve

Going into the Deep: Saints in the Making

Image Courtesy of Allison Hsu

GOING INTO THE DEEP: SAINTS IN THE MAKING

Our journey of discipleship is not only about reaching others for Christ. It is also about allowing our hearts to be transformed by His love. Like Peter, we are called to step out of the boat and trust the voice on the shore. Jesus meets us

in our weakness, forgives us in our failures, and calls us again to follow Him into the deep waters of faith.

THE CALL TO PERSEVERE

Every disciple faces moments of exhaustion, fear, or doubt. The apostles fished all night and caught nothing until they heard Jesus' voice. That same voice speaks into our lives with the same invitation: "Follow me."

To go into the deep is to say yes again and again. It is to keep casting the net even when the catch seems small. Saints are not perfect people. They are ordinary men and women who chose love and faithfulness again and again.

Step into the deep. Though the water may seem daunting, embracing trust and surrender leads to the joy of discipleship and the freedom to become our true selves.

HOLINESS IN THE ORDINARY

Sainthood begins in the quiet spaces of daily life. It takes root in washing dishes, forgiving a hurt, speaking kindly to a stranger, or pausing to pray in the middle of a busy day. Holiness is not distant or unreachable. It is saying yes to God in the present moment.

We often imagine sainthood as something reserved for mystics or martyrs. But God calls every person to holiness: parents, students, workers, neighbors, and friends. The saints remind us that the path to heaven grows from ordinary acts offered with extraordinary love.

ANCHORED IN THE SACRAMENTS

Like the apostles after the Resurrection, we find strength at the shore of every Mass. Christ waits for us in the Eucharist, our food for the journey.

The Eucharist strengthens us when we are weak.

Reconciliation heals us and reminds us that mercy is never far away.

Prayer roots us again in the Father's gaze.

The Church does not send us into the deep alone. She surrounds us with grace.

COMMISSIONED TO LOVE

At the end of every Mass, we hear the words "Go forth." This is our commissioning. We are sent to carry Christ into our families, workplaces, and communities.

This is the rhythm of discipleship:

Gather to encounter Christ.

Be transformed by His grace.

Go forth to share His love.

Every act of forgiveness, kindness, or service is a casting of the net. We may not see the catch, but God does.

THE COMMUNION OF SAINTS

We are not alone on this path. A great cloud of witnesses prays for us. The hidden saints of everyday life show that holiness grows quietly like seeds in the soil. We can ask their intercession, follow their example, and walk the same path they once walked.

REFLECTION QUESTIONS
FROM CHAPTER TWELVE

When has God surprised me with grace when my plans failed?

What fear, habit, or attachment might Jesus be asking me to release so I can follow Him more freely?

How can I live the words "Go forth" this week in my family, workplace, or friendships?

What simple daily rhythm of prayer could help me stay connected to God's voice?

What barrier keeps me or someone close to me from experiencing His love more fully, and how might I help remove it?

Closing Word

This is not the end of the journey, but a beginning. Along the ordinary shores of our lives, Jesus comes to meet us. He speaks our name with patience and love, and once again invites us to follow. The saints remind us that this path is possible. Holiness is not beyond our reach, not because of our strength, but because His grace is sufficient. We are a family, a single school moving together through the waters, drawn both to be caught by mercy and to bear that mercy to others for His name. We share one pilgrimage toward the living stream, the font of life, where our baptism first made us new and named us sons and daughters of our Heavenly Father.

ACTION STEP:
INTO THE DEEP OF DISCIPLESHIP

Return – In prayer, gently place before the Lord any weariness, resistance, or fear. Let Him renew your trust.

Renew – Choose one small, quiet act of love this week: a word of encouragement, an act of forgiveness, or a simple service.

Reach Out – Share a passage of Scripture or a prayer with someone who may need hope.

Pray Simply – *"Lord Jesus, give me the courage to cast into the deep once more."*

Epilogue

As we draw the net closed on this journey of faith, reflection, and testimony, we are reminded of a profound truth: love and discipleship cannot be separated. Just as Jesus called His first disciples to cast their nets into deep waters, He continues to call us today to step out in faith and receive His transforming love.

In our own time, Popes Saint John Paul II, Benedict XVI, and Francis have each spoken of the need for authentic discipleship and what they call the New Evangelization. Even Pope Leo XIV, an Augustinian missionary having served many years in Peru carries this apostolic zeal of evangelization to the Catholic community as head of the Church. To evangelize is simply to share the Gospel, the Good News of Jesus Christ. Each of us knows someone who has drifted, perhaps quietly, from the Church. Now is the moment to walk beside him, to listen, and to invite him back. Jesus calls each of us to tend and feed His sheep. This mission is not for a few; it is the daily calling of every disciple.

The power of love is not found in grand gestures but in the quiet, faithful ways it takes root in the sacrifices we make, the forgiveness we extend, and the courage we show in sharing Christ with others. Love fuels discipleship. It shapes us into vessels of grace, mercy, and hope for a world longing for the light of Christ.

To be a disciple is to live this love. It is more than keeping rules or fulfilling obligations; it is following Christ's example and making Him the center of our lives.

Discipleship calls us beyond comfort, into trust, and into companionship with those who walk beside us in faith.

In Matthew's Gospel with *The Great Commission*, we are reminded that we cannot sit idly by as Jesus commands us to use the power he receives from the Holy Spirit as grace bestowed upon his disciples to go out and make disciples of all nations, "baptizing them in the name of the Father, and of the Son, and of the holy Spirit, teaching them to observe all that I have commanded you."[1]

The stories and reflections in these pages reveal that God works through our lives even through imperfection. Each testimony bears witness that whether we find ourselves unworthy, uncertain, or eager, Christ's invitation remains the same: "Come, follow me."

As we go forth, may we take these lessons to heart. Let us embrace each day as a new chance to serve, to love, and to help lead others to God. Let us cast our nets wide, not for success or recognition, but to draw souls toward His mercy and truth. And let us remember: every act of faith, no matter how small, helps to build the Kingdom of God.

The journey does not end here; it begins anew each day. As you move forward, cast your net with love, not for fish, but for souls, trusting that even the smallest act of faith can draw someone into the embrace of God's eternal love.

---

[1] Mt. 28: 19-20

REFLECTION QUESTION

In what simple way can I cast my net today through a word, a prayer, or an act of kindness that might help someone experience the love of God?

Closing Prayer

Lord Jesus, You are the Good Shepherd and the Fisher of souls. Thank You for calling me to follow You and to share Your love with others.

Grant me the courage to cast my net each day with faith, the patience to walk with those who are searching, and the humility to serve with a heart like Yours. May every word, every prayer, and every act of kindness draw others closer to Your mercy and truth. Bless my journey of discipleship, Lord, and let me never tire of answering Your call:

"Come, follow me."

Amen.

Helpful Resources

Below is a list of suggested resources, both practical and spiritual, to support your faith journey and deepen your daily walk as a Christian disciple. This list is not exhaustive, but it includes many valuable tools and works cited throughout this book.

SUGGESTED ITEMS FOR THE HOME

A PRAYER SPACE

Designate a sacred space for daily prayer and reflection in your home, a quiet corner with a crucifix, candle, or icon that reminds you of God's presence.

Suggested Items:

- Holy Bible: Versions such as the Douay-Rheims, Ignatian Study Bible, New American Bible, or New American Bible Revised Edition. (The most important thing is to read your Bible; an unread Bible collecting dust benefits no one.)
- Catechism of the Catholic Church
- Christian Prayer: The Liturgy of the Hours (or digital versions via iBreviary or Universalis)

- Daily Missal or online access to daily readings via the United States Conference of Catholic Bishops (USCCB)
- Catholic Book of Prayers
- Catholic Book of Blessings
- Books on the Lives of the Saints or their biographies

RECOMMENDED BOOKS

- A Biblical Walk Through the Mass by Edward Sri
- Fire & Light: Learning to Receive the Gift of God by Jacques Philippe
- He Leadeth Me: An Extraordinary Testament of Faith by Walter Ciszek
- Getting Work Right: Labor and Leisure in a Fragmented World by Michael Naughton
- The Power of Silence: Against the Dictatorship of Noise by Robert Sarah
- The Intellectual Life: Its Spirit, Conditions, Methods by A.G. Sertillanges
- Forming Intentional Disciples by Sherry Weddell
- Called & Gifted Resources by Catherine of Siena Institute About Called & Gifted - Catherine of Siena Institute - Colorado Springs, CO
- Against Heresies by Saint Irenaeus
- In the Heart of the World by Mother Teresa
- The Hidden Power of Kindness by Lawrence Lovasik
- Lost in Thought: The Hidden Pleasures of an Intellectual Life by Zena Hitz
- Consecration to St. Joseph: The Wonders of Our Spiritual

Father by Donald Calloway
- Introduction to the Devout Life by Saint Francis de Sales
- Holiness for Everyone: The Practical Spirituality of St. Josemaría Escrivá by Eric Sammons
- The Way, The Furrow, The Forge or Friends of God by St. Josemaría Escrivá
- The Imitation of Christ by Thomas à Kempis
- The Interior Castle by Saint Teresa of Ávila
- Confessions by Saint Augustine
- Selected Writings of Thomas Merton
- Dark Night of the Soul by Saint John of the Cross

PODCASTS AND MEDIA

- Bible in a Year & Catechism in a Year with Fr. Mike Schmitz through Ascension Press
- The Veil Removed: Short film and companion resources on the hidden reality of the Eucharist

Study Guide: The Power of Love & Discipleship

Each chapter includes reflection questions and a concrete action step. Use these for personal prayer, journaling, or small-group discussion.

Chapter 1: Deep Waters, Deeper Faith

When have you experienced moments of doubt or distance from God?

What helped you return to or reconnect with your faith community?

Activity: Write a short prayer asking God to help you cast into the deep this week.

Chapter 2: Swimming Toward Our Mission

Where in your life do you feel you are swimming upstream?

How does your vocation, married, single, priestly, or religious, become a mission?

Activity: Share with a partner one small way you can cast again in faith this week.

Chapter 3: Hearts Transformed by Christ's Love
How has God's love healed your wounds?

What role has the Sacrament of Reconciliation or the Anointing of the Sick played in your life?

Activity: Pray together the Litany of the Sacred Heart or the Examen.

Chapter 4: Casting Nets, Sharing Catches
What small act of kindness has impacted you most deeply?

Do you find it easier to give or to receive God's love?

Activity: Commit as a group to one act of service this week (visit the sick, write cards, volunteer, etc.).

Chapter 5: Living in God's Gaze

How do you recognize God's presence in your daily life?

Which prayer practices draw you closest to Him?

Activity: Pray the Our Father slowly together, reflecting on each line as a personal conversation with God.

Chapter 6: Marriage and Vocation

How did you first come to understand your vocation in life, and how has that understanding grown?

What role does prayer play in strengthening your closest relationships or your family?

How does marriage or family life call you to live less for yourself and more for Christ and others?

How can your home become more of a domestic church where faith is lived and prayed?

Activity: As a family or group, choose one form of prayer to practice this week: grace before meals, a decade of the Rosary, or reading a Gospel passage aloud. Share how it affected your relationships.

Chapter 7: A School of Fish

Who in your life might need a personal invitation into community or companionship?

What does it mean to swim as a school of fish within your parish or faith circle?

Activity: Brainstorm and plan one way your group can strengthen parish unity.

Chapter 8: Called and Caught by Christ

What is your personal testimony of faith?

How do others' conversion stories inspire your own journey?

Activity: Pair up and share your before and after story of encountering Christ.

Chapter 9: The Spirit's Gifts for Mission

Which gifts of the Holy Spirit have you noticed most in your life?

How can you use your gifts more intentionally for the good of the Church?

Activity: Use a Pentecost prayer to pray together for a new outpouring of the Holy Spirit.

Chapter 10: Drawn by the Word of God

How has Scripture guided you through moments of decision or trial?

Which passage of Scripture has most shaped your relationship with God?

Activity: Practice Lectio Divina as a group using John 21.

Chapter 11: Raising Christian Guppies and Lambs

How do you nurture faith in children or younger believers?

What family or parish traditions have helped strengthen discipleship in your community?

Activity: Share one faith tradition and commit to practicing it this week.

Chapter 12: Going into the Deep: Saints in the Making

Which saint's story most inspires you, and why?

What does it mean to strive for holiness in daily life?

Activity: Choose a patron saint together and ask for his intercession in your group's mission.

Glossary of Catholic Terms

This glossary is offered as a simple guide to key terms and sacraments in the Catholic faith. It is not meant to be academic or exhaustive, but pastoral, helping both lifelong Catholics and those who may feel distant or lukewarm toward the Church rediscover the beauty of what we believe.

Each entry highlights the heart of the teaching in clear, accessible language, and many include a short Scripture reference to remind us that our faith is always rooted in God's Word. Whether you are deepening your understanding or taking a first step back into the life of the Church, may these definitions help you see that Christ is always inviting you into a deeper relationship with Him and His people.

Sacramental: Sacramentals are sacred signs created by the Church to help us receive and cooperate with God's grace (CCC 1667). Unlike the seven sacraments, which confer grace by their very action, sacramentals work through the prayers of the Church and the faith of the believer. Blessed objects such as holy water, crucifixes, rosaries, medals, and actions like the Sign of the Cross draw our hearts toward God, remind us of His presence, and help us grow in holiness in the ordinary moments of life.

Sacrament: A sacrament is an efficacious sign of grace, instituted by Jesus Christ and entrusted to the Church, through which divine life is given to us (CCC 1131).

Christ as Primordial Sacrament: Jesus Christ is called the "primordial sacrament" because He is the fullest and original visible sign of God's invisible grace. In His words, actions, death, and resurrection, Christ makes the Father's love present and effective in the world. The seven sacraments of the Church flow from Him and continue His saving presence in history.

Sacraments of Initiation

Baptism: The first sacrament of Christian life. It washes away sin and makes us children of God and members of the Church. This sacrament is rooted in Jesus' command, "Go… baptizing them in the name of the Father, and of the Son, and of the Holy Spirit."[1]

Confirmation: The sacrament that seals the baptized with the gift of the Holy Spirit, strengthening us with His seven gifts to live as mature disciples as demonstrated in the Acts of the Apostles: "Then they laid hands on them, and they received the Holy Spirit."[2] Confirmation is not the end of faith formation but a new beginning in mission.

Eucharist: From the Greek word meaning thanksgiving. The Eucharist is the source and summit of Christian life. In the Mass, bread and wine become the Body and Blood of Christ, nourishing us with His presence and uniting us as one body, as He tells us, "Whoever eats my flesh and drinks my blood has eternal life."[3]

---

[1] Mt. 28:19

[2] Acts 8:17

[3] Jn. 6:54

Sacraments of Healing

Anointing of the Sick: A sacrament of healing for those who are seriously ill, advanced in age, or near death. Through the priest's prayer and anointing with blessed oil, Christ brings peace, strength, forgiveness, and the hope of resurrection.

"Is anyone among you sick? Let them call for the elders of the church… the prayer of faith will save the sick."[4]

Penance (Confession / Reconciliation): The sacrament through which we confess our sins to a priest, receive absolution, and are reconciled with God and the Church. It restores our relationship with God, renews peace in our souls, and strengthens us against future temptation.

"Therefore, confess your sins to one another
and pray for one another, that you may be healed."[5]

Sacraments of Service

Marriage: A sacrament of vocation in which a man and woman are united in a lifelong covenant of love, reflecting the union of Christ and the Church. "This is a great mystery, and I mean in reference to Christ and the Church."[6]

Holy Orders: The sacrament that configures deacons, priests, and bishops for the service of God's people. Through ordination, they are empowered to preach the Word, celebrate the sacraments, and shepherd the faithful in Christ's name.

---

[4] Jas. 5:14-15
[5] Jas 5:16
[6] Eph. 5:32

Prayer & Worship

Adoration (Eucharistic Adoration): Prayer before Jesus in the Blessed Sacrament, often displayed in a monstrance. It is a quiet encounter with Christ, truly present in the Eucharist.

Liturgy: The Church's official public worship, especially the Mass and the sacraments. Through the liturgy, Christ continues His work of redemption in and through the Church.

Ite, missa est: Latin for "Go forth, you are sent." The final words of the Mass remind us that worship sends us into the world as missionaries of Christ's love.

Transubstantiation: The change by which the bread and wine at Mass truly become the Body and Blood of Christ, even though they still appear as bread and wine.

Core Beliefs & Mysteries

Body of Christ: Refers both to Jesus' real presence in the Eucharist and to the community of believers who together form His Church.

Grace: The free and undeserved gift of God's divine life, which enables us to believe, love, and live as His children.

Incarnation: The mystery of God becoming man in the person of Jesus Christ.

>*"The Word became flesh and made His dwelling among us."*[7]

Paschal Mystery: The Passion, Death, Resurrection, and Ascension of Jesus Christ, made present in every Mass. It is the heart of our salvation.

Scripture (The Bible): The inspired Word of God written under the guidance of the Holy Spirit, containing the Old and New Testaments.

---

[7] Jn. 1:14

Church Triumphant : The faithful who have died and are now in Heaven, along with the angels who share fully in the glory of God.

Church Penitent (or Church Suffering): Souls in Purgatory undergoing purification before entering the fullness of Heaven.

Church Militant: Christians on earth who are still striving, struggling, and persevering in their faith against sin, evil, and temptation.

Christian Life & Discipleship

Apostles: The twelve men chosen by Jesus to follow Him closely and spread the Gospel. Their witness forms the foundation of the Church.

Church (One, Holy, Catholic, and Apostolic): The worldwide community of believers founded by Christ and guided by the Holy Spirit, continuing the mission of the Apostles.

Conversion: The lifelong process of turning away from sin and toward God. Conversion is renewed daily through grace, prayer, and repentance.

Disciple / Discipleship: A disciple is a follower of Jesus. Discipleship means living as His student, friend, and witness in everyday life.

Domestic Church: The family, called the "little Church at home," where faith is first taught, prayed, and lived out through love and example.

Mission (Great Commission): Jesus' command to His followers to proclaim the Gospel to all nations.

"Go therefore and make disciples of all nations."[8]

Saints: Holy men and women who lived lives of virtue and now dwell with God in Heaven. Every Christian is called to become a saint.

---

[8] Mt. 28:19-20

Vocation: A personal calling from God to live out holiness through marriage, priesthood, religious life, or single life. Each vocation is a mission of love and service.

Death, Hope & Eternal Life

Funerals: The Church's liturgy of prayer and hope for the deceased. It commends the soul to God's mercy, comforts the grieving, and proclaims the Resurrection. The rite includes the Final Commendation, in which the Church entrusts the departed to the Father, using symbols such as:

Holy Water – recalling baptism and new life in Christ.

Incense – honoring the body as a temple of the Holy Spirit.

Paschal Candle – signifying Christ's victory over sin and death.

References

Biblical References – Scripture quotations are taken from the New American Bible, Saint Joseph Edition, by the Confraternity of Christian Doctrine, 1970.

Catechism References – Citations are from the Catechism of the Catholic Church, Second Edition, published by the United States Conference of Catholic Bishops, Washington, D.C., 2020.

Vatican II References – Documents and excerpts are drawn from official texts available on The Holy See website: https://www.vatican.va/content/vatican/en.html.

Other Sources – Stories and additional texts referenced in this book are used with permission. All images and photographs are either original works by the author or sourced from the public domain, requiring no further permission for use.

Appendix

SURVEY – JOURNEY WITH CHRIST

This self-assessment survey is intended to help you pause, reflect, and notice where the Lord is present in your daily life. There are no "right" or "wrong" answers—only an honest invitation to grow closer to Him.

"Draw near to God, and He will draw near to you."[1]

Daily Prayer Life

How often do I set aside intentional time for personal prayer?
☐ Rarely   ☐ Occasionally   ☐ Several times a week
☐ Daily   ☐ Multiple times a day

What forms of prayer do I practice regularly?
☐ Spontaneous prayer   ☐ Rosary   ☐ Scripture (Lectio Divina)
☐ Liturgy of the Hours   ☐ Other:

How would I describe the quality of my prayer time?
☐ Distracted   ☐ Occasional moments of peace
☐ Regular and focused   ☐ Deep and consistent encounter with God

---

[1] Jas. 4:8

Sacramental and Communal Life of the Church

How regularly do I participate in the Eucharist (Mass)?

☐ Rarely ☐ Monthly ☐ Weekly

☐ Several times a week ☐ Daily

How often do I receive the Sacrament of Reconciliation?

☐ Rarely ☐ A few times a year ☐ Monthly

☐ Frequently

How connected do I feel to my parish or faith community?

☐ Isolated ☐ Occasionally involved

☐ Regularly involved ☐ Deeply rooted in community

Relationship with Jesus

How would I describe my personal relationship with Jesus?

☐ Distant ☐ Searching ☐ Growing ☐ Close

☐ Deeply personal and intimate

Where have I experienced His presence most in recent months?

☐ Prayer ☐ Family life ☐ Work or service

☐ Suffering or loss ☐ Community ☐ Not sure

Living as a Disciple

In what ways am I actively sharing Christ's love with others?

☐ Words / Evangelization ☐ Acts of service

☐ Intercessory prayer ☐ Hospitality

☐ I struggle with this

Which of the following best reflects my current faith journey?

☐ Just beginning ☐ Returning after time away

☐ Actively growing ☐ Serving and leading others

Areas of Growth

I sense the Holy Spirit calling me to grow in (check all that apply):

☐ Daily prayer   ☐ Scripture reading   ☐ Community life

☐ Sacramental participation   ☐ Evangelization

☐ Trust / surrender   ☐ Forgiveness

☐ Silence / contemplation

Discipleship in Action: A Practical Guide

A Practical Companion for Living the Call to Discipleship

Each of us is called to follow Christ not just in word but in action. The following action plans offer simple, concrete ways to return to Christ, renew your commitment, reach out in love, and remain grounded in prayer.

Chapter 1: Deep Waters, Deeper Faith

Action Step: Take the Next Step into the Deep—This week, choose one concrete way to "cast your net" deeper with Christ.

Return – If you've been away from Mass or Reconciliation, set a date this week to go. Walk back into His mercy.

Renew – If you already attend Mass regularly, add one step: arrive early to pray, attend one weekday Mass, or spend 15 minutes in Eucharistic Adoration.

Reach Out – As Fr. Bill did by welcoming me, offer a simple gesture of kindness or invitation to someone who seems distant from the Church. A smile, a coffee invitation, or a word of encouragement may be the net that brings this person closer to Jesus.

Pray Simply – End each day with the tax collector's prayer: "O God, have mercy on me, a sinner."[1] Let humility anchor your heart in grace. Faith is not about diving in perfectly; it's about stepping in again, one act of trust at a time.

Chapter 2: Swimming Toward Our Mission

Action Step: Casting Again with Trust—This week, choose one area of your life in which it feels like you are "swimming upstream." Perhaps this is work stress, family tension, prayer dryness, or financial worry.

Name It – Write it in a journal or speak it aloud: "Lord, here is where I feel stuck."

Surrender It – Place that situation symbolically at the foot of the Cross. Trace the Sign of the Cross over your heart or light a candle before a crucifix.

Cast Again – Ask Jesus for the courage to try again. Take one small, concrete step of faith: make a call, forgive someone, show up to Mass, or carve out prayer time.

Pray Simply – Whisper, "Yes, Lord, I trust You here." Even a small "yes" invites strength into your struggle and turns exhaustion into grace.

Chapter 3: Hearts Transformed by Christ's Love

Action Step: A Prayerful Examen of Love and Hope—This week, make a simple evening Examen, offering it especially for loved ones who are sick or have died.

---

[1] Lk. 8:13

Recall with Gratitude – Thank God for the gift of your loved ones and their example of faith.

Remember in Faith – Reflect on a moment when you witnessed or received the Anointing of the Sick. If you have not experienced either, contemplate Christ as the Divine Physician who brings comfort and peace.

Examine Your Heart – Where do you struggle with fear or doubt about suffering or eternal life? Ask for the grace to take one step closer to trusting God's mercy.

Pray in Hope – Conclude with the Church's ancient prayer: "*Eternal rest grant unto them, O Lord, and let perpetual light shine upon them. May they rest in peace.*" What small step can you take this week to open yourself more fully to Christ's healing presence?

Chapter 4: Casting Nets, Sharing Catches

Action Step: Living the Little Way

Return – Recenter your week on the Eucharist. If possible, attend a weekday Mass or spend ten minutes before the tabernacle, offering your ordinary life to God.

Renew – Choose one daily activity such as work, cooking, errands, caregiving, and offer it as a prayer.

Reach Out – Perform one hidden act of kindness: write a note, wash a dish, or encourage a co-worker. Do it quietly, without seeking recognition.

Pray Simply – End your day with St. Thérèse's prayer: "Jesus, I will seek out a means of getting to heaven by a little way very short and very straight."

Chapter 5: Living in God's Gaze

Action Step: Living a Prayer-Filled Life

Return – Pray the Our Father slowly and intentionally each day. Let its words realign your heart with God's will.

Renew – Turn one ordinary activity such as commuting, walking, or cooking, into a moment of silent prayer.

Reach Out – Ask someone if you can pray for them. Even a simple promise of prayer can open hearts to God's love.

Pray Simply – End each day with St. Thérèse's reflection: "For me, prayer is a surge of the heart; it is a simple look toward heaven."

Notice, Pray, and Share – Ask an elder to share how they've seen God's providence in their life. Reflect on the quiet miracles in your own life and share them, allowing faith to be "caught" through witness.

Chapter 6: Marriage and Vocation

Action Step: Living Covenant Love

Notice – Reflect on how you live and love in your home. Are your words shaped by Christ's self-giving love or by distraction and self-interest?

Pray – Begin or renew a family prayer practice: grace before meals, a morning offering, or a brief Scripture reading.

Share – Discuss one way in which you, as a family, can support one another's faith. Attend Mass together, set regular prayer time, or join a parish event as a family.

Pray Simply – End the day with this prayer of unity: "Lord Jesus, may our family reflect Your covenant love. Teach us to be patient, forgiving, and faithful, that our home may become a true domestic Church."

Chapter 7: A School of Fish

Action Step: Swimming Together in Christ

Return & Renew – Recall your Baptism, Confirmation, and Eucharist as the anchors of your discipleship. Begin each day with the Sign of the Cross, entrusting your life to God's grace.

Reach Out – Extend a personal invitation to someone who may feel isolated. Invite them to Mass, coffee, or a meal. Like the early Christians' fish symbol, let your life be a quiet sign of belonging and welcome.

Pray Simply – End your day with this prayer of unity: "Lord Jesus, help me to not swim alone, but as part of Your Body, the Church. Strengthen my faith, anchor my hope, and increase my charity so that others may find Your love through me."

Chapter 8: Called and Caught by Christ

Action Step: Encountering Jesus in Daily Life

Return – Choose one ordinary area of your life such as work, chores, school, or family time, and consciously invite Jesus into it this week. Say: "Lord, walk with me here."

Renew – Reflect on your personal testimony. Write down one moment when you experienced God's grace, whether through a struggle, healing, or joy, as a reminder of how He has worked in your life.

Reach Out – Share your story with someone: a family member, a friend, or a parish small group. Testimonies, like Peter's encounter with the risen Christ, inspire others to believe that God is alive and active today.

Pray Simply – End each day with this prayer: "Come, Holy Spirit. Enkindle in me the fire of Your love. Renew my heart and guide my steps closer to Jesus."

Chapter 9: The Spirit's Gifts for Mission

Action Step: Sharing Our Gifts for God's Glory

Return – Recall your Baptismal call. Begin each morning this week by making the Sign of the Cross slowly, thanking God for the unique gifts and charisms He has given you.

Renew – Take one step toward discerning your gifts. Pray with Ephesians 2:10 ("We are His handiwork...") or complete a spiritual gifts inventory, asking the Holy Spirit to reveal how He desires you to serve.

Reach Out – Use one of your natural or spiritual gifts in service of another person this week, whether in your parish, family, or workplace. Even a small act of generosity is a step in stewardship.

Pray Simply – End your day with this prayer of surrender: "Lord Jesus, You are the giver of every good gift. Help me to use my time, talent, and treasure for Your glory and for the good of Your Church. Make me a faithful steward of the blessings You have entrusted to me."

Chapter 10: Drawn by the Word of God

Action Step: Letting God's Word Transform Your Heart

Return – Begin or end each day with Scripture. Place a Bible in a visible spot in your home. Before you scroll, check headlines, or fall asleep, read at least one verse, such as the daily Gospel or a Psalm. Let God's Word be your first or final thought.

Renew – Try one new method of praying with Scripture this week. For example:

–   Pray Lectio Divina with a Gospel passage.

— Join others for Morning or Evening Prayer from the Liturgy of the Hours.

— Write a verse that strikes you on a sticky note and place it where you'll see it often.

Reach Out – Share God's Word with someone else. Text a verse that encouraged you, pray a Psalm together before a meal, or invite a friend to join a Bible study. Even one small invitation can draw another soul closer to Christ.

Pray Simply – "Speak, Lord, your servant is listening. Let Your Word be the lamp that guides my path and the lure that draws me deeper into Your love."

Chapter 11: Raising Christian Guppies and Lambs

Action Step: Nurturing Faith at Home

Return – Recall your First Holy Communion. Approach the Eucharist this week with the same love, awe, and reverence you felt that first time. Let that memory renew your gratitude.

Renew – Recommit to at least one family faith tradition this month: celebrate a baptismal anniversary, a saint's feast day, a family Rosary, or go to Confession together. Let traditions become anchors of faith for you and your children.

Reach Out – Make your home visibly Catholic. Place a crucifix, family Bible, or saint's image in a central spot. Let your home silently witness to guests and remind your family that your household is the "domestic Church."

Pray Simply – "Jesus, You said, 'Let the children come to Me.' Teach me to guide my family with love, patience, and courage. Help me nurture faith in my children so they may grow into saints who love You."

Chapter 12: Going into the Deep – Saints in the Making

Action Step: Living Faith Daily—This week, choose one way to plant or water seeds of faith in your home.

Return – Remember your First Holy Communion. Approach Jesus in the Eucharist this week with the same awe and love you felt that day.

Renew – Recommit to one family tradition – pray the Rosary, celebrate a feast day, or go to Confession together. Let it become an anchor of faith.

Reach Out – Place a simple sign of faith such as a crucifix, an open Bible, or a holy image in a central spot in your home. Let it speak silently to visitors and remind your family of your roots.

Pray Simply – "Jesus, You said, 'Let the children come to Me.' Teach me to guide my family with love and patience. Help me raise saints, little by little, through everyday love."

Closing Note

Discipleship is not a one-time choice but a daily decision. By returning to Christ, renewing your commitment, reaching out in love, and remaining steadfast in prayer, you take steady steps into the deep waters of faith – the path that leads to holiness, sainthood, and eternal life with God.

About the Author

Eric is a devoted sojourner of faith, continually guided by the Holy Spirit in living out his baptismal call as a disciple of Jesus Christ. He is happily married to his wife, Angela, and is the proud father of their daughter, Abigail. Together, they serve joyfully in their parish community at St. Joseph Church, where Eric volunteers in various ministries.

He holds a Bachelor of Arts in History with a minor in Philosophy. Eric fully embraced his vocation as a husband and father, finding profound meaning in serving the Church through family life and everyday discipleship.

In his free time, Eric enjoys blogging about his Catholic faith, studying theology and catechetics, particularly through continuing education at the University of Dallas, and pursuing personal growth both spiritually and intellectually. He also values exercise, quality family time, and community service, seeing each as an opportunity to glorify God in ordinary life.